...re fiona Phillips Alain de Botton Donal R
...away Tim Smit... ...n Colfer
...llen White Te... ...gh Abb
...is Riddell Deborah Levy Claire Greaves
...ay Pinnock Tony Husband Ilona Burton M
...tioned — Nicholas Allan Blake Morrison T
...e Nic... ...an Kevin Br
...ding Conn Iggulden Tony Parsons france
...nmore fiona Phillips Alain de Botton Dona
...Harkaway Matt Haig Rachel Joyce Eoin C...
...ae Ilona Burton Tessa Watt Jez Alborough
...Chris Riddell Deborah Levy Claire Grea
...Stourton Shirley Hughes Marian Keyes
...te Nicholas Allan Blake Morrison Tim
...icci french Caitlin Moran Kevin Bridges
...Conn Iggulden Tony Parsons francesca
...e fiona Phillips Alain de Botton Donal Ry
...away Matt Haig Rachel Joyce Eoin Colfer
...na Burton Tessa Watt Jez Alborough Abb
...s Riddell Deborah Levy Claire Greaves
...Stourton Shirley Hugh...
...ed — Nicholas Allan Bla...
...Nicci french Caitlin Moran Kevin Brida

Dear Stranger

Dear Stranger

Letters on the subject of happiness

PENGUIN BOOKS

PENGUIN BOOKS

UK | USA | Canada | Ireland | Australia
India | New Zealand | South Africa

Penguin Books is part of the Penguin Random House group of companies
whose addresses can be found at global.penguinrandomhouse.com.

First published 2015
001

Set in 13.5/16 pt Garamond MT Std, Filosofia, American Typewriter, Goudy Old Style,
P22Dyrynk Roman, Cochin, Miller Roman, Chaparral, LaGioconda (with SpudAFCrisp)
Typeset by Jouve (UK), Milton Keynes
Printed in Great Britain by Clays Ltd, St Ives plc

A CIP catalogue record for this book is available from the British Library

ISBN: 978–0–718–18161–1

www.greenpenguin.co.uk

Our mission at Penguin Random House UK is to make the world a better place, in both big and small ways.

We find the very best stories, writing and ideas from the best writers and we connect them with as many people as possible.

Stories, writing and ideas are at our heart.

Dear Stranger is a collection published by Penguin, part of Penguin Random House UK, to raise money and awareness for our Charity of the Year, Mind.

We wanted our partnership with Mind to go beyond colleague fundraising and volunteering days. We wanted to use our expertise where we could add the most value – by publishing a book.

With *Dear Stranger* we're proud to bring some of our brilliant authors together to share their thoughts on that often elusive subject – happiness.

Everyone at Penguin Random House UK and the fifty authors and bloggers who have contributed to this book have given their time and words for free. All profits from the sale of *Dear Stranger* (at least £3 per copy sold) will be donated to Mind (a registered charity, number 219830).

Mind believes that no one should have to face a mental health problem alone. We hope that these powerful words and illustrations from our authors will bring us all a little closer to that goal.

Contents

CONTENTS

CONTENTS

An Introduction from Mind

*Is it possible to articulate the depths of your feelings
to a total stranger?*

*Is it possible to describe what 'wellbeing' means
to you in just a few hundred words?*

*Can we construct a new language of mental health, wellbeing and
happiness to help us all gain a better insight into ourselves?*

These were the challenges set for some of our country's best-known authors, and their reflections and considerations form this unique collection.

We all have mental health, just as we all have physical health, and this can fluctuate. This is normal, and feeling sad or 'low' is a natural response to some of life's challenges. However, for some people these feelings can escalate, until they affect the way they think, feel and behave.

Some mental health problems are described using words that are in everyday use, for example 'depression' or 'anxiety'. This can make them seem easier to understand, but can also mean people underestimate how serious they can be. For people living with depression, obsessive compulsive disorder, bipolar disorder, schizophrenia or any other mental health problem it can feel just as bad, or worse, than any other illness – only you cannot see it.

Although mental health problems are very common – affecting around one in four people each year – for too long mental health has been taboo: something we don't talk about out of fear, or embarrassment, or a sense that no one else would understand.

For too long, mental health was out of sight, and out of mind. In fact, this very phrase was brought into our language by those who built the asylums 250 years ago. People with mental health problems were taken away to these asylums, built outside of communities so that people went out of sight once they had lost their minds. These asylums were often built with a curved road, unlike the magnificent mansions of the wealthy landowners, who built straight drives so their wealth could be admired for miles around. People with a mental illness instead went 'round the bend' into the abyss of the asylum.

In the 1960s, Mind campaigned for the closure of these asylums. The results were not always smooth, and towards the end of the twentieth century, public attitudes towards mental health worsened as tabloid newspapers declaimed 'axemen schizos' and the 'failures of Care in the Community'. Much of this was ill informed, and based on a small number of tragic incidents. But it served to reinforce the stigma of mental illness and force people into silence and fear.

Thankfully, the twenty-first century is starting to show signs of a fresh approach to mental health. Slowly but surely, we are recognising its importance in our society. We are seeing public attitudes shift and improve, with more and more public figures speaking up about their own experience of mental health problems. And behind these public faces is a movement of tens of thousands of people beginning to talk about their mental health to their friends, families and work colleagues, to their social media networks, and in their local communities.

This people-led movement is being echoed in welcome changes to our society. It seems implausible that just two years ago if you had experienced a mental health problem you would not be able to own your own business, or serve on a jury, or become an MP – we helped to change that. At Mind we welcome this shift. Every day we speak to people who tell us that openness and sharing has helped them learn to live with challenging and life-changing conditions. This is wonderful to hear. But we know that there are still too many people afraid to speak out, or who are trying to seek support and are unable to find it. There are too many people waiting too long for treatment they desperately need, and too many people facing prejudice and discrimination because they live with a mental health problem.

These letters form an inspirational, insightful, uplifting and honest collection of writing on what happiness means to different people and how we can support those for whom happiness feels an impossible goal. Writing to yourself in a diary, to others through letters, or exploring issues in more depth unquestionably has a therapeutic benefit. The letters show an extraordinary level of insight, powerfully expressed. We are reminded of the life-changing impact depression can have, but that even in the depths of our despair, there is hope.

Our authors have also written about their own mental wellbeing and happiness. The results are astonishingly varied – they are incredibly open and honest about the love and support they have received, exploring whether happiness can be found in achievement, or whether it rests in friends and family, or in taking time to appreciate what's around you and live in the moment.

The conditions for any one person's happiness are extremely subjective. Food and the great outdoors features strongly – in fact we know that the benefits of Ecotherapy are indeed good for your mental health, and many local Minds help and support people to do just that. Sometimes, it's a simple activity that makes the difference – knitting, the friendly cat, the black dog that wards off the other Black Dog of depression.

We also explore the concepts of solidarity, succour and solace, pathways to greater calm, and truly knowing yourself as an individual.

Our work at Mind reaches far and wide, supporting nearly half a million people every year. We believe that everyone living with a mental health problem should be able to get the support they need, and be treated with fairness and respect. We provide information and advice to help people make choices about their care and treatment, and we campaign to improve services, raise awareness and increase understanding. Our network of local Minds provides direct support to communities across England and Wales. But there is more to be done.

Which is why we are so grateful to Penguin Random House UK and the wonderfully talented writers who have contributed to this book. Many are household names, and they are joined by some very talented bloggers who have contributed their own stories and experiences.

If you are struggling with difficult thoughts or feelings, I hope this collection will offer you some comfort and remind you that you are not alone. I would also urge you not to suffer in silence. Reach out to those around you, or to your GP, or to an organisation such as Mind. You are not alone and help is available.

I hope you will find this collection of letters as enjoyable, fascinating and helpful as I did.

Paul Farmer
Chief Executive, Mind

PS Some things in this book might be difficult to read if you are feeling a bit vulnerable. Remember you can always speak to Mind via our Infoline – you can call them on 0300 123 3393, text 86463 or email info@mind.org.uk. There's also our supportive online community Elefriends, which can be found at elefriends.org.uk.

1. Fiona Phillips

Fiona Phillips is a television and radio presenter best known for hosting *GMTV* for over twelve years. She has also worked on BBC One's *Panorama*, Channel 4's *Dispatches* and currently works on the BBC's *Watchdog* and *The Truth About . . .* series. Fiona has appeared in two feature films and writes a weekly column in the *Daily Mirror*. She is the author of *Before I Forget*, a frank and open account of her experience of her parents' dementia. She currently lives in London with her husband and two children.

Dear Stranger,

I know you very well. But you are not you right now.
Something has taken you. You have fallen out with Happy.
Happy, your constant companion, has gone. You knew happy.
You had happy. You held hands with happy. You were happy.
You shared happy with me. Your beautiful, wraparound smile
spread the happiness you seemed to constantly harbour
inside yourself. Your glow has shrivelled now. It is tight in
your tummy. Your glow is slow. Soooo so slow. I saw the glow
go. Nothing left to ignite your sunny smile. Your head, once
light and giddy, now seems dumbbell heavy. Your stomach
light. But tight, you tell me. Anxiety somersaulting around:
bashing you inside. Your eyes are full of stinging tears. Those
huge blue eyes. Seeing only sadness. You rub your hands
together. You scratch your skin. You open and close
cupboards, drawers, doors. You switch taps on and off. On
and off. As though your life depends on it. You say it does. You
say you're afraid that something will happen to me. That MY
life depends on you repeating your tortuous routine. You can't
go out. You feel it will be your fault if anything happens to me
when you are out. Or if I am out without you. If you don't turn
the taps on and off, on, off, on off, off and on, something will
happen to me. You are pale. Blue-white. Withdrawn. Shaky.
Isolated. You say no one understands. 'You don't get it!' you
bite when I try and reason with you. 'You can fight it,' I say.
Breathe in through your nose, right down to the shrunken

glow in your stomach. Breathe out. Slowly . . . slowly . . .
slowly. I tell you this. You know it can help. It doesn't. Because
the thoughts are telling you it won't. You allow the thoughts
in. Anxiety taunts and teases, plays, pokes and jabs at you, a
non-entity that has you in its thrall. No one can fight it for
you. Because it does not exist. 'You don't understand,' you tell
me. Because, for you, it exists, it lives inside you. It spreads
like a cancer. And you take to your bed and give in. If I could
fight it off and stifle it and wrap it up and thump it and dump
it, I would. But you are the only one that can toss it away and
watch it slump down the wall like a discarded drunk. The only
one that can walk out of the door and toss it from your
shoulder. The only one that can rage and shout at Anxiety. Tell
it, you will not walk with it. It does not exist like you. It does
not live like Happiness. 'Happiness'. Say it. Happy. Happy.
Happy. Cheerful. Gleeful. Exhilaration. Elation. Jumping.
Whooping. Laughing. Merry. Jolly. Ho Ho Ho.

Oh.

Please don't cry. It's not your fault. Please be happy, not
mugged by sad. Not stamped-on by misery. Not thud-heavy-
headed. My mum used to say: 'As long as you are happy, I am
happy.' But I am not happy because you are not happy. And I
am your mum. You are my little boy. My treasured youngest
son. My sunny little man. Afraid to go to school. Afraid to go
to sleep. Afraid to live your life. Because Happy is missing . . .

2. Martha Roberts

Martha Roberts is an award-winning newspaper and magazine journalist and was shortlisted for a Mind Media Award in 2014 for her mental health blog www.mentalhealthwise.com.

@MarthaRoberts01

Dear Woman in Pink,

You don't know me but I'm sitting on the next table
at the cafe where you're catching up with friends.
I've been sneaking glances, trying to work out
what's going on inside your head. I have to say,
you're doing an impeccable cover-up job; I'm guessing
you've been doing this for a while. You're smiling at
all the right times and trading stories to give the
impression that life is normal. But you can't kid a
kidder – my mental illness radar has gone into
flashing neon overdrive. And it seems to me that what
you'd really like to do is stand up and shout, 'It's all
right for you lot: you're laughing. I don't think I even
know how to do this any more!'
 As I drain my coffee and leave, I want to turn
back and say 'Hi'. I want to talk to you about illness
and desperation and to explain that you're not alone
in your sadness. I want to chat to you about humour,
and how, even in those bleakest of bleak times, it's
possible to reawaken a hibernated joy that can serve
as a lifeline and a vehicle for recovery. I want to tell
you that you can find happiness and genuine laughter
again, even though I sense at the moment you'd think
this is an absurd untruth.
 I can say this because, for a long time, I was you.
Maybe I still am in many ways because mental illness
is, for many of us, a lifelong companion. But in other
ways I've come out the other side and I want to give
you some hope that you can, too.

Humour has always been important to me. A good friend once told me my humour was 'puerile' and looking at the evidence she's probably right. One of my most prized possessions is a remote-controlled fart machine, and when I recently found a fake dog turd in my bedside table I thought a) how funny and b) 'I was wondering where I'd put that.' My appalling capacity to recall just three jokes at any given time means that all of the spaces tend to be devoted to toilet humour jokes (currently top of the list is: 'Have you seen the film *Constipation*? No, you wouldn't have done, it hasn't come out yet.' I know. I apologise). And now that I have a young son, I'm able to indulge both this and our joint love of the absurd so that every day seems to proffer some hilarious belly-laughing moment or other.

However, like you, there was a time when happiness all but left my world, taking humour with it. A series of difficult life events dished out on top of an already latent mental fragility meant that depression felled me like a scythe. As I seriously considered not living any more, humour seemed perilously far away. Like you, I had moments when I smiled, but this was transient and cultivated largely for the benefit of those who I felt couldn't cope with my marrow-deep despair.

It seemed like I didn't laugh for a good three years of intense illness (possibly longer). And even after diagnosis with bipolar, I became terrified of laughing in case it signalled hypomanic 'joy' before depression – a confident spring followed by a late, biting frost. But after a while, I chanced upon a convalescent's way of cajoling humour back into my life. I found that familiar comedy shows with scenes I could recite verbatim reminded me that I had once found things hilarious and could, therefore, do so again. I watched *Friends*, *The Office*, *The Vicar of Dibley* and *Miranda* – rather than new comedy in case I failed to find it funny and ended up even more depressed. And in doing so, I discovered it reconnected me to my intrinsic love of humour and shone as a ray of hope in the hopelessness of depression. Even now, I find that these familiar funny TV scenes serve as a salve when I'm wobbling. Alongside conventional approaches (meds, therapy, plenty of sleep and time with friends) they remain part of my 'self-care' package.

Slowly but surely, humour has reappeared in my life, frequently in the guise of irony or 'gallows' humour that I think can spring from being mentally unwell. I've seen dark things, mainly the black-lined inside of my own mind, and at times hung on to life by a spider's thread, suspended over an abyss that seemed more home than hell. It's this brush with life's end that I believe reconnects people like us to life's intense joys. Sadly, we all know too well that for some the pain turns out to be terminally corrosive. But I count myself one of the lucky ones. Now, I see humour all over the place, from the realisation that just above my bottom is no place to consider having a 'This too shall pass' tattoo to my eight-year-old asking if he'd be a 'good specimen' if there was a 'Crufts for boys'.

This is the prize, the 'treasure in the trash' that people like us can mine for so triumphantly when we've spent so much time sifting through the detritus of despair. I want you to know that like me, your humour, your laughter, your happiness, hasn't really gone, even though it may well feel that way right now. It's there for you to quietly cultivate so that, slowly but surely and in your own time, it can hopefully give you some succour in your sadness. Each person's experience of illness is so very different but I like to think that you, too, will find yourself laughing again.

Maybe I'll see you doing this, from the heart, at the same cafe not so long from now.

Love and strength, from one stranger to another.

Martha

3. Francesca Martinez

Multi-award-winning Francesca Martinez is the only woman to win the Open Mic Award at the Edinburgh Festival, and has since become one of the top comedians of her generation. As well as touring internationally with sell-out runs around the world, Francesca is a TV and radio regular, making popular appearances on such varied programmes as *The News Quiz*, *The Jonathan Ross Show*, Ricky Gervais's *Extras* (in a role written specially for her), *Newsnight*, and *Channel 4 News*. She is also the author of *WHAT THE **** IS NORMAL?!*, a very funny and moving celebration of learning to be happy with who you are.

Dear . . .

Sometimes life feels like shit. It throws you on the rocks.
Wave after wave crashes over you, until you lie broken and
gasping for air. Loss, illness, heartbreak, death. And at their
core, an epicentre of blood-red pain that throbs like a
lighthouse at night. On and on. As regular as a heartbeat.
No inspirational quotes or platitudes will dull the aches,
though they may make you want to punch something.
Hard.

A pain-free life doesn't exist. And if that's what you're
after, try not to love. Because love will always come to an
end and that end will hurt. When my grandma died, I wept
for weeks. Misery wrapped me in its cold arms and there I
stayed. Then, it dawned on me that I was devastated simply
because I loved her. Had I not loved her, I would not have
shaken with tears. I mourned her because she meant so
much to me. That pain would have been less if she'd been
less loving, less giving, less affectionate. And I realised that,
in some way, this grief was the price I had to pay for love. I
clung to that thought as if to a life raft and began to see my
sadness as a privilege. I was lucky to have known the kind of
love that makes you howl at the stars. And I would choose
this pain again and again over never knowing what it feels
like to love.

I couldn't rush my grief, nor did I want to. I knew it would
ebb away slowly with time. Happiness is to be cherished and

pursued, but life is multi-coloured and this was my time to cry and mourn and grieve. It was part of being human and alive and connected, and I felt lucky to know what it was like to feel great sadness. Some day I won't be able to feel anything so I'm grateful to know that, while I'm alive, I can feel. Feeling is a beautiful thing. Most stuff in the universe can't feel or cry or laugh, and I have to pinch myself that I won the lottery: I got to exist.

It's so important to know what is worthy of your tears, and what isn't. When life doesn't throw the heavy stuff your way, rejoice. Don't waste those tears on trivialities. So much suffering comes from living in a culture that makes people feel not beautiful enough, not rich enough, not successful enough. But beauty, wealth and success are just social constructs designed to disempower people. They are ways of getting us to conform and consume. These pressures exist solely to enslave us economically and psychologically. These values are toxic, and lead to a life wasted on chasing empty goals and obsessing over what others think of you. I adopted them in my teens and was reduced to a gibbering wreck. But it doesn't matter what anyone thinks of you. Just focus on what you think of yourself. Accepting yourself is an act of civil disobedience.

The pain caused by society's superficial goals is real. But you can free yourself by rejecting them and remembering what is truly valuable – your experience of life. Don't let anyone else hijack the wonder of being alive. You won't happen again. I was made to feel that my body didn't work properly, or move correctly or look normal. Then I realised that we are all unique. There is no perfect body. We each get our own shell and those shells give us life. They are the most amazing things in the galaxy. And we should love them for every minute they keep us breathing.

Every day, when you wake up, try to remember what it took for you to be here. The chances of us bursting into life are practically zero. The cold, dark expanse of space could have been lifeless and the dust of distant stars could have formed something else. Yet, here you are.

Francesca

4. Rachel Joyce

Rachel Joyce is the author of the *Sunday Times* and international bestsellers *The Unlikely Pilgrimage of Harold Fry*, *Perfect* and *The Love Song of Miss Queenie Hennessy*. *The Unlikely Pilgrimage of Harold Fry* was shortlisted for the Commonwealth Book Prize and longlisted for the Man Booker Prize. Rachel Joyce was awarded the Specsavers National Book Awards 'New Writer of the Year' in December 2012. Rachel Joyce lives with her family in Gloucestershire.

This is a story about a yellow flower and a woman who didn't like the look of herself and also happiness. It may seem unlikely, those three together. But sometimes that's the way with stories.

There was a time in my life when things were tough. You know how it is. And the hardest part was that I couldn't seem to find a way to help myself. You maybe know how that is too. Everything was flat and empty. I couldn't imagine laughing. I only wanted sleep. Then something happened.

One day I walk out of my house and there is a wild marigold, growing right by my front door. It's so golden and fine the petals look as if they have been shredded with a pair of tiny scissors. I've never noticed this plant before. I haven't even spotted a little green shoot. Until now my front step has been neat concrete. And then - pop. Yellow flower. It's like the sun coming out. As if the flower is saying, *Here I am.*

I don't know why I love that flower so much but I do. Every time I open my door, there it is. Smiling at me. I persuade myself that I'm not alone any more because that flower is there, and so I water it. Then I begin to worry. Supposing I go and tread on it? After all it's in a stupid place. I end up putting a Post-it note reminder on the front door (*Don't tread on yellow flower*). Maybe I become over-protective, I don't know. It's possible to do that with happiness. To get so afraid of losing it, you don't dare move.

Anyway. My aunt comes to stay. She's heard I've been having a hard time and I think she wants to help. I love my aunt though I find her eccentric. Once when I was a child I noticed that all the photos in her flat had little bits cut out of them and so I asked her, Why? And she said, 'Oh I always look dreadful in photographs. I snip myself out.' And for a long while I had this image in my mind of a cupboard full of snipped-out mug shots of my aunt and I don't know why but that thought really tickled me.

My aunt arrives with her suitcase and I take a nap because I get so tired, and when I wake up I go to find my aunt and she's sitting outside in a sort of housecoat and a turban - she's going a little bald - and yes, you've guessed it. The marigold has gone.

'Where's my yellow flower?'

'I did some weeding.'

I follow her eyes to a little pile of roots and stems and there at the top is my flower and already it is dying. The colour is fading. It's not even yellow any more. I am so angry I want to shout.

'It's rampant,' she says. She widens her eyes and shakes her head knowingly as if she has just saved my life. 'You need to invest in proper weedkiller. These days you can get it with a special spray nozzle.'

Again I follow her eye line. And then I see. Specks of yellow all over my garden. Even in the walls, the gate, the pavement. That flower is everywhere. I think of my aunt, wilfully taking scissors to photographs because she has some misplaced idea she should be absent. I think of my yellow flower that I spotted one day and which made life special when really it was all over the place, if only I'd looked.

And I think, happiness is a slippery bugger.

Maybe it would be better if we just sat down and stopped trying so hard.

What's so funny, asks my aunt?

5. Donal Ryan

Donal Ryan is the author of *The Spinning Heart*, which won the Guardian First Book Award, Book of the Year at the Irish Book Awards, and the 2015 European Union Prize for Literature. It was shortlisted for the International IMPAC Dublin Literary Award and longlisted for the Man Booker Prize and the Desmond Elliott Prize. His second novel, *The Thing About December*, was shortlisted for the Kerry Group Irish Novel of the Year. Donal holds the 2015 Arts Council Writer-in-Residence Fellowship at the University of Limerick, where, with Joseph O'Connor and Giles Foden, he teaches Creative Writing. He lives with his wife Anne Marie and their two children just outside Limerick City.

You don't know me but I know some things about you. That you buy your lunch every day in the same deli as me. That your hand always shakes as you count out your change at the counter. That you get flustered when there are people behind you in the queue: you feel you're holding them up; you redden, and apologise, and your shoulders hunch even more, as though you're trying to hide inside yourself. Your voice is almost a whisper. I know that you're gentle, and fearful, and sad.

I think you live somewhere near where I work. Sometimes I don't see you for weeks at a time. When I see you again you're paler and slighter than you were before. I think I know where you are those times. I hope you're given comfort there.

Be happy is a senseless exhortation. *Be* makes far more sense. Live. Survive, please. Happiness is of the same nature as ideas, insight, inspiration: it can't be willed into existence, you have to wait, and listen, and be open to it. You have to accept that it's possible to not feel lost, or afraid.

I saw you once on a mountain path, a few miles from the city, coming down as I was going up. You seemed taller there, in the open space. I don't think you recognised me but still you looked at me and smiled. And I was surprised by your smile, and grateful for it, and glad to think of you as a person who smiles at strangers. Such small, perfect kindnesses, aggregated and compounded, could change the world. I stood beside a great metal cross at the summit that day and whispered a prayer for you into the sweet updraft, and let it be carried away to the ether, to join with all the other swirling entreaties and requests for intercession. That you would know how rare you are, being gentle, and kind. That you would know how precious you are, having been plucked from infinity and fashioned from the dust of stars. That you would know that life is the universe's way of seeing itself, of feeling; that you would remember, when the darkness closes around you, that you are the light.

I don't know you, but I know your hand shakes as you count out your change in the deli. I don't know you, but I think I know something about how you feel. Some days I see you in the street, head down, shoulders hunched, picking your steps carefully, making way for rushing people, avoiding cracks in the pavement. Some days I see you in the mirror. Sometimes I open my mouth to speak and I hear your voice.

I want to put my hand out to stop you some day and tell you that I don't know you, but I think about you every day, and I want you to survive, to set your face to the sun, and the wind, and the rain, to always walk head up and straight-backed through this world, and to love yourself.

6. Matt Haig

Matt Haig's first novel for young readers, *Shadow Forest*, won the Blue Peter Book of the Year Award and the Gold Smarties Award. He is also the author of various adult novels, including the bestsellers *The Last Family in England*, *The Radleys* and *The Humans*. Reviewers have called his writing 'totally engrossing', 'touching, quirky and macabre' and 'so surprising and strange that it vaults into a realm all of its own'.

Dear Twenty-four-year-old me,

I am writing this letter from the future.

Time-travel may or may not be possible, but I like to feel I have already read this letter, when I was your age. That somehow, in some hidden way, you (me) always knew it was going to get written.

So what do I say in this letter?

Well, I suppose, I start with this:

You don't actually do it. That killing yourself thing. I know, you want to do it. You keep trying to summon the courage to do it. But you don't. You won't. And this is good.

No. Really. It is good.

You are still going to die of course, somewhere down the line, but not right now.

Oh, and I don't want to lie. It's not going to be easy. The next three years are going to be the three worst years you will know. There will be many days where you will feel like you do right now, days where the anxiety is so strong there is nothing you can do to calm yourself.

There will be days when you feel a sense of doom about the slightest things – the sun slipping behind a cloud, the infinite emotional trauma of what shoes to wear. One day you will be in the car, sitting next to your father, and you will feel an incredible weight and want to open the door and jump out onto the motorway, in the hope that the

large lorry you can see in the mirror will run you over.
There will be days when even words don't mean
anything. When the pain you feel is beyond language and
will hardly be able to speak or read.

But listen.

And listen hard.

You are ill. The thoughts you are feeling are symptoms
of an illness. And, like many illnesses, this is an illness
most people recover from, or at least learn to live with.
You will always be a depressive but you won't always be
depressed.

Also, and this is the really hard thing to understand.
You will one day be thankful. Thankful for this
experience of being ill.

Since getting ill I've read a lot of writing about
depression. R. D. Laing said that 'breakdown is often
breakthrough'. And this is how it was for you. All that
pain you are feeling is actually change. Think of the terror
a caterpillar might feel in the darkness of its cocoon and
try and realise that what feels like pain can actually
sometimes be change.

When you come through the other side of this you will
feel different. Make no doubt about that. Depression
draws a line. It separates lives into eras. It gives you a BC
and AD of your own life. You will remember what you did
and who you were before the age of twenty-four but you
will be remembering a different person.

Right now you are in between those people. You have
fallen down a ravine, falling between the gap between
who you are and who you want to be. But you must
know, you have to know, what I am telling you now: you
will experience days better than you have ever known.

You are in total shadow, but that darkness will one day

make you appreciate the glowing light we take for granted in normal life.

This pain will protect you, because every time you suffer in the future you will be able to tell yourself you felt this pain and you survived it. And so, for all your future selves, for all those days where you will thank yourself for not killing those countless moments of quiet wonder.

Those quiet human routines that you will know again. And also those moments of unknowingness. Of just being. Of being that most unlikely of unlikely things, a living human, on the scariest and most miraculous planet we will ever know.

Stay strong. Let the pain happen, because it will anyway. And also a trick: when you start to panic, let yourself. This fools anxiety. Invite it in, and leave the door open, and you will find it will leave. And be careful with that third glass of red wine.

You will make it.

You don't think you will because you are listening to your depression. But depression lies.

I am the future. It isn't all hunky-dory. But it is life, and life is always worth it.

Stay strong and you will make it. In fact, you already have.

Yours sincerely,
Me (You).

7. Philippa Rice

Philippa Rice is an artist who works in a number of different mediums including comics, illustration, animation, model-making and crochet. Her first book, *Soppy*, is a collection of comics based on real-life moments with her boyfriend. Her other work includes the collage-based webcomic *My Cardboard Life*. Philippa grew up in London and now she lives in Bristol with illustrator Luke Pearson.

8. Naomi Alderman

Naomi Alderman's first novel, *Disobedience*, won the Orange Award for New Writers and the *Sunday Times* Young Writer of the Year. Like her second novel, *The Lessons*, and her third, *The Liars' Gospel*, it was broadcast on BBC Radio 4's *Book at Bedtime*. In 2012, Naomi was picked by Margaret Atwood to work with her on the Rolex Arts Initiative, and in 2013 she was chosen by *Granta* for their once-a-decade list of the Best of Young British Novelists. She is a frequent radio broadcaster, writes a regular column for the *Observer*, is Professor of Creative Writing at Bath Spa University and is the co-creator and lead writer of the hit smartphone app *Zombies, Run!*

I don't know how much I rate happiness.

I mean it's fine, happiness, it's alright. It's actively nice, obviously, really enjoyable. When the day happens to come along every now and then that I just feel delighted with the world, with the sunshine, with all of the lovely things that life has to offer, if I happen to feel that all day long, I take it and enjoy it. But, I don't know, I tend to feel that we make a bit too much of it these days? Because you can't be happy all the time, I mean you just can't, and if you could, you probably wouldn't want to.

If you've ever experienced grief, you'll know how real it is, how true and how important it is to sit with, not to try to plaster over or 'make it better'. Mourning for a loved one means that you loved them, that you miss them, that every time you remember it's really true that they're gone you feel it. It would be a kind of blasphemy to insist on happiness in those shell-shocked days and weeks after a death.

Or at the end of a relationship, it can be right to feel grief. God knows I've done my share of walking-in-the-rain-crying, and it's not that it feels *nice* exactly, but that it feels necessary. Or when you witness injustice: would it be right to feel happy, somehow not to experience that boiling rage which can prompt you to act on that inner prompting to do something extraordinary which, in sunnier moments, you might just let slip by? Or when you contemplate some of the wretched things that people have done to other people, continue to do today everywhere in the world (you don't need me to spell them out. We all know what I'm talking about): one might not feel the need to cry over them, but there's a kind of dishonesty in thinking that one could always, or even mostly, be happy in a world where these things are going on.

I honestly think that happiness can so easily shade into blindness, into lack of compassion. It's when I remember how sad I have been, how anxious, afraid, lonely, angry, despairing, hopeless, it's then that I break through my own shell of arrogance and privilege. It's there, I think, that love dwells. Not in happiness, but in the acknowledgement of all that is human.

There's that song that was the big thing last year, which said we should clap our hands if we felt happiness was the truth. It was everywhere, and every time it came on in a shop or a restaurant or a cab, I kept wanting to talk back to it, and say, instead:

- Clap along if you feel that happiness is just one of a range of human emotions which, in their breadth and complexity, go to make the beautiful richness of life and each of which is true if it's with you right now.
- Clap along if you feel that the late capitalist system insists on happiness, which it ties to a range of consumer products in order to firstly make us feel bad for not being happy all the time and then secondly to claim that we *would* be happy if only we had this product or service, which all makes us more willing to buy more stuff.
- Clap along if you feel that the pressure to exhibit happiness is ironically making us more miserable.

Not that there's anything wrong with happiness. But it needs to know its place.

9. Yuval Noah Harari

Prof. Yuval Noah Harari has a PhD in History from the University of Oxford and now lectures at the Hebrew University of Jerusalem, specialising in World History. His research focuses on broad questions, such as: What is the relation between history and biology? Is there justice in history? Did people become happier as history unfolded?

He is the author of the international bestseller *Sapiens: A Brief History of Humankind*. In 2012, Harari was awarded the annual Polonsky Prize for Creativity and Originality in the Humanistic Disciplines.

What Happiness Is

Discussions of happiness all too often bog down in a semantic quagmire. Different people use different definitions of happiness, or they fail to provide any definition at all. Yet it seems that in the early twenty-first century, a single and very concrete definition of happiness has come to dominate our economy and, to a lesser extent, our science. According to this definition, happiness is pleasure, or even more precisely, it is pleasant sensations in the body.

This definition goes back to the philosopher Jeremy Bentham, who in the late eighteenth century argued that nature subjugated humankind to two absolute masters: pleasure and pain, and they alone determine everything we do, say and think. Beyond pain and pleasure, there is no good or evil. What was a radical idea in the days of Bentham, is today the orthodox scientific view. According to the life sciences, happiness and suffering are nothing but bodily sensations. Nobody suffers because he lost his job, lost a fortune, or got divorced. The only thing that makes people miserable is unpleasant sensations in the body. Conversely, nobody is happy because she got a promotion, won the lottery, or found true love. The only thing that makes people happy is pleasant sensations in the body.

This is why the pursuit of happiness often leads us nowhere. For no matter what we achieve in the outside world, our happiness remains in the hands of the biochemical system that regulates our bodily sensations. And our biochemical system was not shaped by evolution to produce a constant stream of pleasure. Winning the lottery or finding love may trigger a flow of pleasant sensations in the body, but sooner or later the pleasant sensations will turn into unpleasant ones. Consequently, people may feel depressed even in the midst of affluence and success. You can live in a beautiful house, with a new car, a fat bank account, a great job, a loving spouse – but as long as the sensations in the body are unbearable, life can still be hell.

Since the problem is the unpleasant sensations and the biochemical system that produces them, it cannot be solved by changing the outside world. The only solution is to gain control of our biochemical system, and re-engineer it to ensure a constant stream of pleasant sensations. This is the Brave New World that science, in alliance with consumerism, is trying to create for us.

An alternative view of happiness equates it not with pleasure, but with meaning. We are happy when we are engaged in a meaningful activity, and when we feel that there is meaning to our life as a whole. The key to happiness is to find what is our role in the great cosmic plan – and fulfil it.

Unfortunately, to the best of our scientific understanding, there is no great cosmic plan, and life has absolutely no meaning. As Shakespeare put it, life is a tale told by an idiot, full of sound and fury, signifying nothing. Any meaning that humans imagine their lives have, is just that – something that they themselves imagine. If happiness is meaning, then in order to be happy we need to deceive ourselves. Quite a depressing thought.

People might still find happiness in *feeling* that their lives and actions have meaning, but this is merely another kind of pleasant sensation in their own bodies. If so, the only thing we need to tell the scientists working on re-engineering our

biochemical system, is to have the system produce that particular kind of pleasure.

A very different approach sees happiness not as a particular kind of sensation, but as freedom from the pursuit
of sensations. The life sciences are correct in identifying
body sensations as the key battleground of happiness. But
they misinterpret the role of these sensations. They think
that pleasant sensations are happiness, when in fact the
pursuit of sensations is the deep root of suffering.

Because we ascribe so much importance to the pleasant
sensations, we spend our lives pursuing them. Whatever
we do, from fidgeting slightly in the chair to waging world
wars, is driven by this pursuit. Whenever we experience an
unwanted sensation, we react with dissatisfaction. Even
when we experience a pleasant sensation we react not with
satisfaction, but with craving for more. And if we happen to
get some sensation of pure bliss, it doesn't last for more
than a moment before it disappears, and we have to start
pursuing it all over again. We may live like that for ninety
long years, constantly chasing these ephemeral and meaningless vibrations, and in the end we have absolutely
nothing to show for all that effort. That is slavery.

Freedom from this pointless rat race may be achieved by
seeing our sensations for what they are: fleeting and meaningless vibrations. Once we realise the meaningless and
ephemeral nature of all sensations, what would be the point
of trying to get one particular sensation rather than
another? For thousands of years, wise people of all cultures
and traditions emphasised that in order to be really happy,
you must know the truth about yourself and your place in
the world. Knowing yourself as waves of evanescent sensations, just allowing the waves to come and go without trying
to freeze them, chase them, or drive them away – this is
happiness.

This third approach to happiness may be the most insightful. But it is extremely hard to practise. Pursuing pleasant sensations comes far more naturally to us. After four billion years of evolution, we are simply addicted to it. So in all likelihood one of the great projects of humankind in the twenty-first century will be to re-engineer humans in such a way that they will experience more and more pleasant sensations all the time. Will it succeed? Will it really make us happy? We will see by and by.

10. Ilona Burton

Ilona Burton is an assistant producer, writer and mental health campaigner with lived experience of anorexia, bulimia and depression. She has written extensively on the subject for the *Independent* and is the author of *Anorexia: The Essential Guide*.

To Whoever,

Happiness is a weird old thing. It's oddly instilled into us as children; all those 'and they lived happily ever afters', always the last we hear of the (mostly pretty messed-up) characters. We presume everything's rosy, but we don't know for sure. Silly, really. Idealistic poppycock that fails miserably to set us up for a life that could well be full of misery. It's probably why, with the exception of *Fantasia*, my parents didn't let me watch Disney.

You might be a naturally happy person. You might get on with everyone you meet and be one of those lovely people who never sees the bad in anyone or anything. If that's you, well done, please tell me how.

Thinking about happiness too much can make you unhappy. I think we're somehow programmed to focus more on the things that make us unhappy, or perhaps that's just an easier thing for us to comprehend because we take too much of the good stuff for granted. I think if we took more time to stop and think about how lucky we are and focus on those things we often forget to appreciate, we'd be happier. You and I should try that.

But there are times when happiness really does seem impossible, incomprehensible even. It could be a few weeks of darkness during times of stress or after an upset, but for some it continues and grows and the thought of being happy becomes a foreign concept. It could happen to anyone at any time and you or someone you know will feel deeply unhappy as you sit here now, reading this.

Depression, or any form of prolonged sadness, doesn't really have a good side, but if there is anything positive to be taken from it, it's that we can learn from experience. We can't make it go away, but if we can find a way to get from wanting to end it all to taking one day at a time and getting through, then that's something. It's incredibly sad, but the truth is that for some people, the happiest they feel is when they wake up and not hate themselves for being alive. For some, that's progress – a step closer to happiness.

People – nursing assistants, consultants, psychologists – used to ask me, 'Do you think you'll ever be happy?' What a question. At the time, I was a depressed young woman living on an eating disorders unit, being forced to do everything I had spent years telling me would make me even unhappier. I would cry over a glass of orange juice and self-harm when rain meant I wasn't allowed to go on my (prescribed) twenty-minute walk around the hospital grounds. I was a long way from happy, and there were many times that I didn't want to get better at all. I'd rather be thin and miserable than healthy and happy – or so I thought. I didn't think happiness was for me, I just wasn't designed that way.

I thought about that question a lot, in the end deciding that I would never be the 'happy' that you see in some people. Those impossible people who bound into work on a Monday morning, always beaming no matter what. Wanting that kind of happiness when, like me, you're not designed that way, won't get you any closer to being happy. Never compare your happy to anyone else's, but look out for what makes you smile and surround yourself with it as much as you possibly can. If you don't force it, it will grow.

Things change. Priorities change. I was in hospital still, but my first niece was born and over time, I realised that I had to change too. I didn't want to be the auntie who was stuck in the revolving door of the mental hospital. You can't make yourself happy and nobody can make you happy, but you can work with the positive things that surround you to help find your way out of unhappiness.

It's playing 'Peep-bo' with babies, it's running in the rain, singing out loud, being ridiculous with friends or having a duvet day with the Disney films you weren't allowed to watch when you were little. It's ordering Domino's and not giving a shit. It's taking time to be you. It's putting yourself first every now and then, because no matter what you think or feel, you really do matter.

Here's something to remember: everything is temporary. When all you can feel is pain or worthlessness or emptiness or nothing at all, know that it's not for ever. You might feel stuck or trapped, it might even seem as though there is no way out or that the only way out is to cease to exist, but feelings, like everything else, are just temporary. Always cling to that thought.

Take care,
Ilona
X

11. Rowan Coleman

Rowan Coleman lives with her husband and five children in a very full house in Hertfordshire. Despite being dyslexic, Rowan loves writing, and has written eleven novels. She juggles writing with raising her family, which includes a very lively set of toddler twins whose main hobby is going in the opposite directions. When she gets the chance, Rowan enjoys sleeping, sitting and loves watching films; she is also attempting to learn how to bake.

Dear You,

You don't know me, but here I am writing to you anyway,
which is an idea that I rather like. You and I, we have
never met and yet there is this common bond between us
that makes it possible for us to connect in this way. We
are both Human Beings, and because of that we each face
the same struggle, the same desire to be happy, to be
contented, to feel successful. But although life is a journey
that we both have to travel, all too often it feels like we
have to travel it alone. It may feel like that, but we don't
have to. There is always someone out there who is ready
to take our hand.

Two summers ago, I was lying on my office floor
crying, when I suddenly thought, 'Hang on, this isn't
right. This isn't how a person is supposed to live their
life.' It was on that bright, summer morning that I realised
I hadn't been able to feel actually, truly happy for a very
long time.

I was a happy child, my mum used to say. I'd laugh to
see a pudding roll, and for the most part I've been a
reasonably happy adult, or, at least, about the same as
anyone, with ups and downs, highs and lows. And then
suddenly, for no reason particularly at all, those two
summers ago, it all became too much. It felt like my world
had turned into a constant night.

The sun could be shining, the sky could be blue, but

still, all around me, I felt the darkness, pressing in, invading my lungs, weighing heavy on my chest, pushing me down. And when you are in that place it's impossible to try and imagine a sunrise, it just is.

Other people might tell you to snap out of it, or pull your socks up, or think about everyone in your life who needs you, and honestly those people are trying to help. It's just I don't think they understand what depression is, how all-invasive it is, like a weed that will not stop growing in your heart and mind. No one who suffers from depression wants it, or gets it because they can't be bothered to try hard enough to be happy. It chooses you, not the other way around.

But here's the thing, the very, very important thing.

It will pass. And you will feel happiness again. Happiness, in all its bright, beautiful glory, is on the way, travelling steadily towards you, just as surely as you fight every morning to get out of bed.

If you just *know* that happiness is something you *will* feel again, then the sadness becomes bearable, treatable, endurable. Because all you need to be able to live through those periods of seemingly endless dark is to know for certain that the sun *will* rise, it always rises, eventually.

It's not optimism you need; don't feel bad if you are not one of those people who can see a glass half full. It's not even hope.

No, what you need, what we all can have, is that *certainty*. We can be certain that when things feel entirely and eternally terrible, they *will* get better. Happiness is inevitable.

The trick is learning to recognise it when it comes. Maybe it's the feeling of your child resting their head on your chest. Perhaps it's seeing your dog chase a gaggle of geese into the canal, as if she were the world's greatest warrior – and then, moments later, running away from the swans. It might be some really nice freshly baked bread and butter, or an afternoon on the sofa watching *Brief Encounter*. Happiness can come when you are crying your eyes out, when you are at work. It creeps up on you, surprises you, suddenly fills your heart with purpose.

For me, happiness isn't a full orchestra of noisy joy. It isn't being rich, or being famous, or being popular or successful. For me, happiness comes in tiny, nebulous bursts of gloom-piercing sunbeams.

And when those moments of happiness come, live them, breathe them. Reach out and hold them, recognise them, in those precious moments make sure you take note of every aspect of how you feel and remember it. Experience it, embody it, memorise every little detail of it, write it down if you have to, so you have evidence, so that you know *for sure* that happiness, however fleeting, can be yours, just as surely as it can be anyone's. That you have been happy, and you will be again.

Even though life is a journey we mostly take on our own, it's our very humanness that means we are part of something much bigger than just ourselves. We are part of a huge crazy wonderful family that, even though it has a mass of faults, will never ever stop taking care of us, as long as we let it. It's OK to ask for help, it's OK to need it. Needing other people is part of what makes up capable of being happy.

With best wishes,
Rowan Coleman

12. Ellen White

Ellen White is a sixteen-year-old blogger, writer and mental health activist. Her blog, 'Ellen's OCD Blog', won the Mind Media Award for best blogger in 2014.

You deserve happiness. This may seem a little outright coming from a stranger, but it's true. However I won't define happiness for you, that's what is so special about it. Nobody's happiness is identical. Maybe you're happy because you got full marks on a test, or maybe you're happy because you didn't let an intrusive thought gain control over you. Both situations, even though they may be polar opposites, create similar feelings. An internal warmth, a feeling of satisfaction. Maybe utter disbelief at what you've just achieved, who knows! However, an important thing to remember is that we shouldn't judge people on what they are happy for, even if what they are happy about seems silly to us.

Maybe at this moment in time, happiness feels like a distant memory. A new day doesn't seem like a blessing, but more of a curse. You're stuck in a whirlwind of emotions, or maybe even no emotions at all. It's as if the canvas on which you've painted your entire life has been smudged and all the colour has been washed away. You feel blank. Your paints have all turned to shades of grey and your paintbrushes are broken. At the same time you can see others painting with bright, vibrant colours, encapsulated in a whirlwind of vibrant hues that symbolise all aspects of life, which makes you feel even worse when you look down at your own paint palette and all you can see is grey. That's how I would describe the feelings of depression. As if all the colours have been washed out of your life and it feels like you'll never get them back. I know at this point in time it's difficult to believe that things will ever get better, that you are destined for sadness, but I promise that won't be the case. I've been there, had my whole world turn grey, but I've also found that spark again. Rekindled that flame inside of me and began to experience life again. Yes, it was one of the hardest journeys I've ever had to go through in my life so far, but I can safely say it was the most rewarding. I think going through any mental health condition makes us a stronger individual. I feel as though happiness takes on almost a new meaning, because it may have been absent from our lives for so long. However, it is important that you don't set yourself an expectation for a specific type of happiness. That will be discovered in time.

Reach out. This is quite possibly one of the most daunting things anyone has to do, but it's so crucial. People make up those colours in your paint palette. Without them, the colours would never be as vibrant. There are people out there to help you. My psychologist has changed my life in ways I never thought possible. To have that place of security and trust meant the world to me. I feel that is what you need. I believe that nobody is ever without the capability to experience happiness again. We all deserve happiness. I just feel like we can get cloaked with a veil of depression, OCD, Trichotillomania, Bipolar and so many more, that the colours of life can be blanked out. It's with the help of the mental health community, that could be family, friends, psychologists, online friends, anyone that can help you find your true self again, that we can lift that veil from over our eyes to reveal the true colours on our paint palette again. We had never lost them in the first place, people on the outside could always see our potential, it's just when times are extremely tough, we can often forget that through no fault of our own.

What I will leave you with is something that I hope you will remember. Throughout life the opacity of colour on your canvas will fade the older the brush strokes get, but they will never disappear. The happiness that once resonated full beam will always reside there. Take time to notice and cherish these good memories, as they are easily forgotten about. Don't let the faded colours distort the amazing memory that may lie behind it. However don't forget to keep adding new splashes of colour as you go through life. You have control over your own canvas. You are unique, your life is precious. You deserve happiness.

Yours sincerely,
Ellen

13. Abbie Ross

Abbie Ross moved from London to North Wales aged two and lived there until her family moved to West Gloucestershire when she was twelve. She has written about her childhood 'living the dream' in 1970s Wales in her memoir, *Hippy Dinners*. Abbie has a Psychology degree from Cardiff University and lives in Bristol with her husband and children.

You don't know me, so you might think it's just not on, me sending you this; keep your nose out where it's not wanted, you know, that kind of thing. I'm not what you'd call a letter writer, so this is new to me, as I don't doubt you can already tell. I'm having a go at being bold, that's the thing: stepping out of the comfort zone; *vive la différence* as they say on the other side of the Channel. If you don't like what I have to say, please just scrumple this up and chuck it straight in the bin. Job done. I won't be offended, I promise.

Who are you? I bet you're thinking, and what the heck are you doing writing to me? Well, my name's Enid, and I live at the other end of the street, in the new build next to Bargain Booze. What do I look like? Not so memorable; mousy hair, all my own teeth still, in a dark-green coat usually, with or without my see-through rain cap, depending on the weather. You'd be more likely to remember my dog Cracker I should think. He's a cheeky little scamp, black with a white patch over one eye. About a fortnight ago he took a shine, as they say, to your Spaniel, in the park, right bang in front of the sandpit. Do you remember? He's tiny, half your dog's size. Hats off, ten out of ten for effort, that's what you said. We had a good laugh about that.

We walked back to the Raleigh Road entrance after that; and that's when you told me that you'd lost your wife; last May, I think you said it was. You said you were having a bench put up in her memory, at the end of the park where the rose bushes are; she was a big fan of roses you said. We were still chatting when Jenny Jackson from number nine's black Lab – Jasper he's called – shot out of the pond and jumped all over us; a great big ball of mud and slobber. 'DOWN, BOY!' Jenny shouted, too late though, your beige slacks were covered by then. I don't know what's got into him, he's not himself, she said; he's usually so obedient. Blocked anal glands, that's what she put it down to, she was going to tackle them herself when she got home, save having to take him to the vet. The chat sort of fizzled out after that; I'm just not sure where you go after anal glands.

It was my birthday yesterday. Bear with me, it all ties in, I sometimes detour round the houses but I get there. My son, Gerald, took me to see Barbra Streisand at the O2. Stupendous – the only word for it. Barbara would have been more than enough for me, but the festivities didn't finish there; post concert, Gerald had another trick up his sleeve he whisked me off to my favourite Chinese restaurant! Generous to a fault, that's Gerald. It's the added extras I love about that place, you get refreshing slices of orange with your coffee and a fortune cookie each with the bill. *Seize the day*, that's what my cookie said, so I thought well there you are then, that's what I'll do, I'll write to him. Go for it! Gerald said; that's his motto these days. He's learning the trapeze, that's his latest. He's even got himself a turquoise leotard, it's long-sleeved and quite thick fabric, but ever so revealing even so. That's the kind of person he is lately, nothing scares him, not even heights or leotards.

What I wanted to tell you in the park that day, before the muddy ambush, was that I'm a widower too, like you. I lost my husband, Bert, five years ago. He's got a bench too, it's by the pond; you can find him sandwiched in between Josephine Hughes and Brenda Jones, who were both big fans of the ducks. Bert always liked the moorhens best; their yellow legs and red beaks give a nice dash of colour on a grey day in London, that's what he used to say.

After Bert passed, my friends kept telling me it would get better; time heals et cetera et cetera. I know how you must feel, they would say. I'm not an angry person, Gerald will vouch for that, but that really used to get my goat. What did they know? Their husbands were still with them, right as rain; they didn't have the first clue! So when you said to me, ever so quietly, as you were dabbing the mud off your trousers with your hanky, when you said that you thought you'd never find happiness again, what I wanted to say, what I should have said right then, is that you might not think it, but bit by bit, in the tiniest little ways, happiness, I think, finds you.

The smell of the jasmine in my sunroom, that's what I noticed first. It's not for everyone, it makes some people feel a bit queer, I know that; but to me there's no smell in the world that can beat it. My morning coffee hitting the spot again, the sight of Cracker running for his stick, ears flapping about all over the place, that's what first made me smile. Nothing much to write home about, small things, but big, in a way: molehills, if you like, that became mountains.

I've learned a lot from Gerald, and the way he lives his life. Loneliness is the enemy of happiness he says, and he knows all about loneliness, living with HIV. He's not about to pop his clogs, don't think that – nowhere near – they can do such a lot with medicine these days, I'm sure you no doubt know. The diagnosis has changed him though, and for the better he always says. He doesn't dilly dally or faff about now; life is for grabbing with both hands he says. *Fortune favours the brave*, his cookie said. 'There you go, Mum,' he said. 'I'm brave enough already, you eat it, it's your turn now.' So I did.

Sincerely,
Enid Brown

14. Giles Andreae

Award-winning children's author Giles Andreae has enjoyed huge success with his Purple Ronnie and Edward Monkton characters. He is also the author of a number of celebrated picture books for children. He lives in London with his wife and young children.

the knitting gorilla

After six beautiful daughters, the Big Gorilla finally had a son.

'You will grow up to be big and fierce, just like your daddy!' he said proudly.

But the Little Gorilla grew up to be . . . small . . . and gentle . . . and not like his daddy at all.

And what he liked doing most . . . was knitting.

'The shame of it!' said the Big Gorilla. 'knitting!'

'Daddy,' said the Little Gorilla one day. 'I've made this special sweater for you. Look, there's a banana on it!'

As the Big Gorilla looked, an unfamiliar feeling rose in his chest and he knew that he would love that little son of his for ever.

At first, the other gorillas taunted him. 'Sweater boy!' they jeered. 'Feeling chilly?'

But the Big Gorilla held his son's hand tight and walked calmly past them.

Soon, the gorillas got used to the sweater. Then they began to respect it. And finally . . . every gorilla wanted a sweater.

And the Little Gorilla has not stopped knitting since.

15. Conn Iggulden

Conn Iggulden is one of the most successful authors of historical fiction writing today. Following the *Sunday Times* bestsellers *Stormbird* and *Trinity*, *Bloodline* is the third book in his superb new series set during the Wars of the Roses, a remarkable period of British history. He has written two previous historical series.

When my children were born, my concern was that my elderly parents might die before the babies were old enough to actually *know* them. I'd met only one of my grandparents and I'd always felt the loss. My own earliest memories don't go back beyond the age of five or six, so I only hoped the old folks could hang on until the youngest were about that age.

As the years passed, it occurred to me that the idea had already failed. My parents were no longer the people they had been. My children could never know the people I had known.

It's almost too obvious to say, but the physical self is part of the self. My mother was a highly intelligent woman for example, an English and History teacher of great charisma and rock-solid faith. The sweet and rather forgetful old lady my children ran to hug was not the woman of prodigious physical strength I had known, who chased me down a road in my teens when I was rude to her. In short, old age is a kind of death. You retain the same name and you do look roughly similar, but – and please take a moment to consider this – it isn't *you* any more.

In the flush of your youth and strength, part of who you are is wrapped up in the ability to drink, run, catch, stay up all night, remember a hand of cards, oh, a thousand other things. If you lose them to old age, you lose yourself. It's not just wrinkles. Edgar Allan Poe said: 'Sleep, those little slices of death. How I loathe them.' But, honestly, it would have been just as true to say '*Days*, those little slices of death . . .'

We have to gloss over this truth, for all the pain and discomfort it would cause to accept it: the man or woman who goes to sleep is not the same one who wakes. 'I think, therefore I am' is true for *whoever wakes up*. Not really a test, then. Luckily, human beings are very good at rejecting uncomfortable things. I feel like the same man. My toothbrush is where I expected it to be and I still have that gas bill to pay – I am clearly the same man.

We can see the changes and even understand that all change is an ending. If I suffer a head injury and lose my empathy, or my sense of smell, I am another man, with a slightly different set of characteristics. It does not matter if he thinks he is still me. He isn't.

Big changes are not always strokes, or cancer, or even chronic pain, which changes entire personalities over enough time. Change happens in slow increments, too slowly to see, like a child growing, or hair vanishing from a man's head. Yet the hair is just as gone in the end. There is change and there is death, in each and every day of being alive. We just don't like to see it.

The reason I began this letter to you in such a way was because I am not the young man I was. What I am about to reveal is *his* belief, *his* thought, from a quarter of a century ago. Most of that younger man is lost to me. I hardly even understand how he thought, but I do remember one thing he said.

I do not agree with it now; I have grown softer in body and in emotion. Age *does* soften; the years can be a thumb, rubbing at edges until we are all smooth. The man I recall had a capacity for ruthlessness, with his own life and others. He could jump from a moving train. He could laugh at broken teeth. He did not care, overmuch, for mornings after.

This is the thing he said. This is the thing I said:

If I had to choose, between happiness and achievement, I would choose achievement. I would live my life in misery and cast a vast shadow from a great light. I say that cows in the field are happy – and I aim higher than bovine contentment. I believe that happiness is not enough to be a man's ambition. I understand that for some who have been broken, who are broken still – simple happiness, simple peace is more than they can dare to dream. For those souls, it might be enough, but I am *not* broken and it is not enough for me.

Now of course, I am a father and I have died a thousand times. My younger self of hard bone and bright self-belief would surely scorn the older me. Age and the growth of empathy do tenderise the meat somewhat: happiness does not seem such a second prize to me now. I might consider I had learned a little wisdom on the subject, if not for that whispering voice. I am not him, but . . . I was him. He is no longer here to ask what he has learned.

And finally, this weaker modern me would have you smile and relax a little before you turn the page. Perhaps my dear old Irish mother was right all along – and happiness should be our aim in life. It might be that writing books, or building temples like the London Shard, or even bringing irrigation to a desert is *all* just a kind of graffiti, a desperate attempt to leave a mark, without the perspective to see how transient it all is. Perhaps the only true thing of value in the entire universe is your own family. It's possible. I just wish I could be certain.

Conn Iggulden

16. Seaneen Molloy-Vaughan

Seaneen Molloy-Vaughan is a Northern Irish writer on mental health. Since 2007, she's written the blog 'Mentally Interesting – The Secret Life of a Manic Depressive' (http://thesecretlifeofamanicdepressive.wordpress.com) about her experiences of living with bipolar disorder. It was dramatised for Radio 4 in 2009, and won best radio drama at the Mind Media Awards. She's also written for BBC Ouch, the disability site, as well as the *Guardian*.

You don't know me, but I was scared that I'd be suicidal on my wedding day. I know, the happiest day of my life, as everyone kept telling me it would be. From every person in my life to every shelf in every newsagent's. 'Imagine! A summer bride!'

But I couldn't imagine wearing my wedding dress, nor the fussy clucking of my sisters at its hem on that August day. I couldn't imagine walking down the aisle towards the man that I loved, nor his smile, his eyes, though they were as familiar to me as my own.

I couldn't imagine anything, because there was nothing in the world to imagine any more. But there must have been a 'before'. A 'before' this blackness descended on me. I knew there was a 'before'. A before when I'd been so euphoric at my friend's funeral that I pole-danced on the Tube to the wake. That 'before' seemed as unreal now as the idea of there ever being an 'after' this. This felt like the only reality there ever was, ever had been.

I forced myself awake every day, missing my alarm, again. I had to do what people did; to eat and dress and go to work. I dragged my body onto the bus, threw it onto the seat like luggage. Voices and engines droned on as my face floated in the glass, the world slipping past, roads, people, whole seasons. After a while, I stopped searching for a why in the window. There was no why. Then there stopped being a 'when'. It was bipolar depression. It wasn't a revelation, nor was it a relief. It just — was.

Spring. Blossoms and pink, snatches of green. Sunlight making the glass-face crease. Unslept eyes searching for the empty seat. Diagonal across them, willing itself to be invisible. The mechanical whirr of wheels and wails from babies getting caught in the snares of my never-silent brain. Barbed words on repeat, in a thousand different voices recorded over the years. I took them from the bus, to work, back home, to bed, to tomorrow. They were an endless, skipping soundtrack, distorting the words of everyone around me.

But I did begin to recover. One morning, I took the bus, sat down and moved my bag to my knee. A lady sat next to me, and said she liked my hair. And there was silence in my head. Her words were solid and real. I smiled and said thank you. I sat up straighter, and leaned my head against the window.

Summer, lush and verdant and speeding by. Brightness. It was hot, but someone had opened a window. The breeze rushed in. I looked around me at the faces of other passengers. Not parroting drones but people just going places. And there are so many places in the world to go to. In so many Julys, and I wondered, without dread, how many more I'd see.

I took a long lunch break, everything feeling both urgent and slow at the same time. I drank coffee, not out of necessity, for the first time in months. The stupor began to lift – then fall again – but each time, it lifted itself a little higher. And higher, with sensation creeping back into my skin, and my mind getting a little quieter and quieter, letting the summer sounds trickle in. The ordinary world began to take over the din.

I didn't expect to be happy again. I found it hard to recognise what happiness was. I felt nervous acknowledging it at all, as though if I did, it would disappear. But it came back in moments, and part of me once again, piece by piece. Laughing unselfconsciously at a joke. The small, secret places that you find alone, and keep to yourself (a silly street sign, a patch of flowers growing from bricks). And the magazines did lie. I didn't coast along my wedding day in a wave of joy. It was, as the other happinesses were, moments. Walking down the aisle, it wasn't joy I felt, but recognition. After had come. And there was no why.

17. Genevieve Taylor

Genevieve Taylor is an author and food stylist who splits her time between food writing and creating beautiful food for photography. She lives in Bristol with her husband and two children, along with her chickens ('the girls'), two dogs and two cats. When she's not in the kitchen she can usually be found outside – gardening, walking or cooking in the fresh air. Genevieve is the author of *Marshmallow Magic*, *A Good Egg*, *How to Eat Outside* and *STEW!*, *SOUP!* and *PIES!*.

A hug in a bowl – warm rice pudding on a winter beach picnic.

Happiness often comes in little parcels and, as a food writer, for me, bursts of taste and smell are high up there as life's principal pleasure-givers. The simple things will always work best – a perfectly ripe tomato eaten on a warm day, juice and seeds exploding on first bite, the intensely heady aroma as you inhale deeply from a newly opened bag of coffee, the homely, comforting smell of a chicken roasting in the oven or that first sip of a much-deserved glass of wine at the end of a long day. These moments are so fleeting they barely register at the time, yet I know they enrich my world immeasurably.

More tangible as lasting happinesses are the small adventures I find myself on with my family. The first outdoor picnic of the year, on a bright day at the end of January, is one that will remain etched in my mind for years to come. We left the city at dawn and sped down the motorway to hit the beach, one of my favourite places to be whatever the weather, but especially uplifting on a sunny winter's day. The plan was to light a fire and over it simmer a cauldron of rice pudding whilst we frolicked around keeping warm, hunting for elusive fossils, searching for *the* perfect stone for skimming and chucking sticks and seaweed into the surf for the dogs to fetch.

As kids, it was always a comfort to eat rice pudding, the sort of thing Mum would give us as a treat if we'd been poorly. And if you never tried it cold, straight from the tin, you've missed a trick – the sort of non-guilty guilty pleasure we should all indulge in from time to time – but for the real deal it really has to be homemade. You can obviously cook rice pudding in a pan on the hob in the warmth of your own kitchen, but dare I suggest that getting a little out of your comfort zone and taking it further afield might double, even treble, the pleasure it brings? If ever there was a food that provided a hug in a bowl, surely rice pudding would be it, and this is the one I will remember eating over all the others that have gone before.

Rice pudding is the simplest of things to make and, to make it outside, I weigh it out and bag it up before leaving home to minimise the fuss. On that day I cooked it in my sturdy Dutch oven (a heavy cast-iron lidded pot) hung over a fire pit on a tripod, but a sturdy old saucepan will do – provided it has no plastic handles.

Vanilla rice pudding, for about 4 hungry adventurers...

You will need: 1 litre milk, 150g pudding rice, 60g granulated sugar, 50g butter, 1 tsp vanilla extract.

What to do: Simply measure out all the ingredients into a large sturdy Ziploc bag, sealing it up tightly, squeezing out as much air as possible. Give the bag a little squash and squeeze to get everything nicely mixed and pack inside your Dutch oven or old saucepan and load it into your car. Alongside it, pack a fire pit and a tripod to hang it off, as well as a bag of charcoal, a fire lighter and some matches to get the fire started.

Once you are at your destination, get the fire lit pronto (a good rice pudding takes time to cook to perfection), and send the kids off to gather driftwood to add to the fire to keep them gainfully occupied. Open up the Ziploc bag and empty the contents into the Dutch oven or pan, covering with a snug-fitting lid. Hang over the fire, where it will take a couple of hours of gentle puttering away over the fire to thicken to a creamy consistency, with pretty much no attention bar the odd stir towards the end of cooking.

If you are cooking it in a saucepan, rest the pan on a coolish part of a grill hung over your fire, or even directly into the embers at the very edge of the fire, but be prepared to give it a little more attention as it cooks as it may stick if it gets too hot.

Once the rice is tender and surrounded by a thick, creamy sauce, spoon into bowls or mugs and tuck in.

This is a dish best eaten piping hot, just as we did on our winter beach picnic, and it was just as good as I imagined it would be. Cold hands wrapped around enamel mugs of a warm, delicious pudding, a smile on our faces and a glow in our tummies, it was the perfect end to a lovely day. And definitely the best rice pudding I have ever eaten.

18. Thomas Harding

Thomas Harding is a journalist who has written for the *Sunday Times*, *Financial Times* and the *Guardian*. He is the best-selling author of *Hanns and Rudolf* and the forthcoming *The House by the Lake*. In the following pages Thomas writes about a particularly happy family memory. It is one of the memories which led him to write *Kadian Journal*, a poignant and inspiring record of grief following the death of his fourteen-year-old son, Kadian. The scene takes place at Arundel Castle, close to the Harding's home in Hampshire.

It's a glorious cloudless day. The high summer's sun shines warm as we walk up the wide paved path towards the castle.

There are eleven of us: Deb and me, plus our two kids, Kadian and Sam. We are joined by our good friends Jane and Greg, with their brood of five, Edy, Ella, Harry, Laurie and Grace.

We had chosen to spend the day at Arundel Castle on the English south coast, partly because it was located halfway between our homes, and partly because we thought it would be fun to explore this magnificent medieval structure, festooned as it was with rambling ramparts, crenellated turrets, secret passages and luxurious bedchambers.

Having paid our entrance fees, we stroll through the tapestried hallways, which in days gone by were lit by torches, past a long line of knights standing erect in their shiny suits of armour, before climbing to the very top of the highest tower. There we survey the expansive view: the village below with its maze of narrow streets and stone-faced houses, the winding river and ancient bridge, the lush green fields beyond dotted with little white sheep, and further still, the grey-blue of the sea, speckled by white-sailed yachts and, on the horizon, enormous container ships, poised on their way from here to there.

Once the tour is complete, we are jettisoned into the castle's grounds. With less urgent purpose, we head out across the finely trimmed lawns. Harry chases Laurie between the rose beds. Grace shows off her recently learned cartwheels, legs a perfect V. The rest of us trail behind, quiet after the grandeur that is now behind us.

I cannot remember who starts it. Maybe it is me, or Greg, or Edy, or Kadian. But from one moment to the next, we are transformed from upright tourists into a horizontal jumble of arms, legs and bodies.

I do remember that I am at the bottom of the heap, squashed under the weight of Sam, then Kadian, then Ella and Edy. The wriggling stops for a moment as Greg, all six foot four inches of him, lays down on top. I let out a groan, acutely aware of his body mass, but appreciative that, though my chest is further depressed, Greg is careful not to press down too hard.

Next comes Harry, Grace and Laurie, jumping on to their father's back, completing the tower of laughing, writhing, wriggling limbs. The two mothers stand to one side, approving, appreciating this other, castle of love.

This, then, is my moment of happiness, a beacon of raw, unvarnished joy, burning bright, which I can head towards when the light darkens and I am lost.

After a few brief, precious seconds of giggles and yelps and general raucosity, the moment passes.

Someone calls out, 'That's enough'. Another cries, 'Whose foot is that?' A third grumbles, 'Get off!' We unscramble, the heaving mass becoming separate once again.

And with the glow of the tussle still ripe on our faces, we set off back to the cars parked outside the castle's walls.

19. Jez Alborough

Jez Alborough is the author and illustrator of over forty-five books for children, including the bestselling *Duck in the Truck* series and the *Eddy and the Bear* trilogy which was made into an award-winning animated television series.

In 2000, Jez created *Hug* – a powerful and touching book of only three words about a baby chimpanzee called Bobo who loses his mum. It was chosen by Oprah Winfrey for her recommended reading list. Bobo went on to star in two more classics: *Tall* and *Yes*.

Jez's latest creation is *Nat the Cat*, who features in a new rhyming series with Billy the Goat and Hugo the Hare.

Nat the Cat jumped out of bed
with a smile spread halfway round her head.
She packed a picnic snack to share
with her hoppity friend – Hugo the Hare.
With a smile on her face and picnic in paw
Nat **KNOCK KNOCK KNOCKED** on Hugo's door.
'**HUGO**,' she called, 'are you ready to go?'
but then, oh dear . . .
Hugo said: '**NO!**
My ears are all floppy,
I've lost my hop
I want to get going
but my body says, "Stop".'
It's hard to feel bright on a day like today,
when the sky is so dingy, dreary and grey.
'I'm sorry,' he said, 'I don't want to be rude,
but Hugo is not in a picnicky mood.'

'Never mind, Hugo,' said Nat the Cat
and she gave Hugo's head a **PAT**, **PAT**, **PAT**.
As Nat skipped away, Hugo felt strange
the feelings inside him started to change.

His feet, which had stopped,
developed an itch.
His ears, which had flopped,
now started to twitch.
They began to point upwards,
they lost their flop,
then suddenly Hugo went

HOP

HOP HOP!

The grey in the sky had decided to stay
but the grey inside Hugo
had all gone away.

The inspiration for *Nat the Cat's Sunny Smile* was an event which happened many years ago when I was walking to a studio I had in Covent Garden. In the morning rush to work I passed by a woman who gave me the most lovely, beaming smile. I remember being slightly shocked at this unexpected gift – why had she smiled at *me*? As I turned the corner I realised that I was now smiling too; she had passed on her smile to me. It was this ability to affect others with our emotions that I wanted to explore in the story of Nat the Cat making a picnic to share with her friends. To make the story work I found that I had to be careful to reflect the psychology of what it means to help someone who is feeling sad.

When Nat meets Hugo and finds that he is in a sad mood she doesn't try to change him by telling him to just stop being sad and come to the picnic. She honours him by listening to his description of how he feels. Then she acknowledges him verbally by saying, 'Never mind, Hugo.' Whenever I read this aloud in schools I make sure it is said with a gentle, caring tone. You can see from the kind expression on Nat's face that this is not a dismissive statement meaning 'get over it', but rather a compassionate reaching out from one animal wishing to give comfort to another in need. I felt it was important that there was physical contact too; touch is a big part of connecting with others, whether it be a hand stroked, a hug or a gentle pat on the head as happens here.

The way I see it is that Hugo's happiness was always inside him; Nat's love just helped to bring it out.

20. Caitlin Moran

Caitlin Moran was brought up on a council estate in Wolverhampton where she was home-educated, wore a poncho and had boys throw stones at her whilst calling her 'a bummer'. She published her first novel, *The Chronicles of Narmo*, aged sixteen and became a columnist at *The Times* at the age of eighteen. Her multi-award-winning bestseller *How To Be a Woman* was published in twenty-five countries, was a *New York Times* bestseller and won the British Book Awards Book of the Year. Her second novel, *How To Build A Girl*, was a *Sunday Times* number one bestseller, and she now co-writes the hit Channel 4 sit-com *Raised by Wolves* with her sister, Caz. At one point she was Columnist, Interviewer and Critic of the Year – so in your face, 'bummer' boys.

Oh, baby – I know the address to put on this letter. It is 'To The Dark Place' and I know it because I have been there. I have walked down the gloomy, empty roads at 4 p.m. in January, to that disused warehouse with no windows, and walked around that room. I have slumped on that floor.

Sometimes I would get drunk there – but it's no place for a party, and the wine soon tastes of vinegar. And anyway, the hangover makes the floor seem harder, as you lie on it, mouthing, blankly, 'I want to die' into the dust. And it's not like you've totally lost your sense of humour. You will laugh at yourself as you do this.

'This is like the Low Point in a film, where everything is lost for the hero,' you will say to yourself, lying face-down on the floor, dramatically tear-stained. 'This is Frodo and Sam in Mordor; this is Maria von Trapp, when the Nazis trap them in the nunnery. I am the Ghostbusters just as the Stay Puft Marshmallow Man stamps on that church. A giant Stay Puft Marshmallow Man is stamping all over my cathedral right now. My cathedral is squashed.'

So this is good. You're still on speaking terms with yourself. You're trying to make you laugh. You're making yourself aware of other people who have been in bad places – and then got out of them again. You're looking for inspiration. You're doing the right thing.

Because this is the most important thing, when you're in the Dark Place – to be aware of how you are talking to yourself. What is the voice in your head? Who is it? Who's running your internal monologue? Are you still echoing things your parents said to you, or someone at school, or a cruel lover? Are the things other people said to you – years ago, decades ago – still butting in on your conversation with you?

Here's a good way to tell if the voice in your head isn't one hundred percent you: are you polite to yourself? Are you kind? The key to good relationships, studies have found, is to say five positive things for every negative, or critical, thing. This is how harmonious spouses stay together; how good working partnerships thrive. Five compliments for every 'But could we just . . . ?' or 'I don't like it when . . .'

And what I have learned is that you must not treat yourself any less courteously than you would a loved one, or a team-mate. You cannot spend days bitching at yourself, saying, 'You are worthless', 'You said a stupid thing', 'You always make these same mistakes, and your knees are fat. Indeed, the mistake you *keep* making is to have fat knees. You are a terminally fat-kneed clown.'

You would not stay silent if you saw someone being so repeatedly vile to someone else – if someone spoke to your brother, or sister, like this. You would fight them. You would ride into battle on a *horse* against them. And yet, look at all the things you are saying to you – the unkind whispers as you dress, or sit on the bus. You are so *rude* to yourself. No wonder you have ended up here, alone, in this warehouse – at an impasse with yourself, once again.

So here's how you get out of that room. You must treat yourself as a loved one, or team-mate. Or pet. Imagine how you would treat a pet – how you talk to it in a gentle voice; make sure it's warm; delight in giving it treats, or taking it for a walk.

Become your own pet. Choose what you would be. Select your daemon. It's a delightful hobby to have – being your own pet. For many years now, I have been a small, charismatic dachsund called Eric. I *love* Eric. I can be unabashed in my love of Eric – his stumpy legs, his gleeful leaping. Oh, I treat Eric so well! I make sure I walk Eric every day, for I have found he gets morose if he's cooped up. He needs an hour of fresh air, regardless of the weather – he needs to look up at the sky, and have his heart race when birds fly overhead. He needs to gallop around a bit, woofing – which I disguise as jogging, and going 'AHHHH!' at the top of steep hills. He needs regular meals, and a good night's sleep, and to be stroked, curled up on the sofa, watching musicals.

Eric loves jaunty clothes – he's got a red bobble hat and a duffel-coat he feels very dapper in. And whenever Eric gets fraught, and thinks he's having a nervous breakdown, I give him a cup of tea and a biscuit, and he almost invariably feels happier. It is amazing, over the years, how many times you will confuse 'having a nervous breakdown' with 'just needing a cup of tea and a biscuit'. So I always have a big biscuit tin – for Eric.

And because I am kind to Eric, we do not fear visits to the Dark Place now, when they come – although so much less frequently than they used to, before we were together. When we're in there, we never stop talking to each other – reminding each other that we have been here before, and there is always a moment where the door – which we could not find before – opens up, and we can walk out again, into the sunshine. And we do not fear that we know we'll go there again – because the Dark Place is not all bad, you know. We learned to trust each other, in the Dark Place. We bonded, in the empty place. We've had some quality time there.

And we also know why we end up there, now: because depression takes a layer of skin off, so you feel more of the world than most people. But, as I explained to Eric, that sentence changes, depending on how you say it. We feel more of the world than most people. WE FEEL MORE OF THE WORLD THAN MOST PEOPLE. That's *amazing*. That is why we end up in the Dark Place – but it is also why we cry with joy when we listen to David Bowie, and are obsessed with the moon, and can stare at the redness of cherry-juice on our fingers and imagine a whole world that is cherry-juice-red – with stained-glass trees and frosted crimson grass, and tiny, bright birds that fly out of scarlet oyster shells. Every day *is* a fight – the highs are high, and the lows are low. You are rarely lukewarm. But you and Eric – you are witnesses together. You are not alone, alone.

21. Blake Morrison

Blake Morrison is the author of the bestselling memoirs *And When Did You Last See Your Father?* (winner of the J. R. Ackerley Prize for Autobiography and the *Esquire* Award for Non-Fiction) and *Things My Mother Never Told Me* ('The must-read book of the year' – Tony Parsons), the acclaimed novel *South of the River* and a study of the disturbing child murder, the Bulger case, *As If.* He is also a poet, critic, journalist and librettist.

Dear Clarke Carlisle,

You don't know me, but I read the memoir you
published in 2013, *You Don't Know Me, But . . .* More
importantly, you spent several years of your football
career at Burnley, the club I used to watch as a
teenager and still support; I was at Wembley in
2009 when Burnley beat Sheffield United in the play-
off final to win promotion to the premiership and you
won the Man of the Match award. Even before you
retired, you were famous for being intelligent and
articulate, qualities not always associated with
footballers. You've appeared on *Countdown* and
Question Time; been chair of the Professional
Footballers' Association; worked as a commentator for
ITV; and made a documentary called *Is Football
Racist?* Quite the Renaissance Man.

    You were in the news again late last year after being
knocked down by a lorry in Yorkshire, an accident that
left you with internal bleeding, a broken rib and a
shattered left knee. Except it now turns out it wasn't an
accident; that you threw yourself in front of that lorry
because you wanted to die; and that after leaving Leeds
General Infirmary you were admitted to a psychiatric
unit in Harrogate. It's brave of you to have brought this
out into the open; mental health issues aren't often
discussed in the sporting arena. And I'm heartened to
read that you're now on the road to recovery.

    Still, it's distressing to think how unhappy you'd
become – unhappy enough to try to take your own
life. You'd lost all sense of purpose, you say. And

something that seemed amusing when it first happened – strangers stopping you in the street and asking 'Didn't you use to be Clarke Carlisle?' – made you doubt you'd anything left to live for. I'm tempted to say we've all been there – that everyone must have had similar moments of despair. But I'm not sure that's any consolation.

No one knows the secret of happiness. But I did once write a poem that expresses my idea of it, and though your version might be less rustic, and less sedentary, I'd like you to have the poem. What it says is that happiness is real but transitory – that we experience it briefly and then it's gone again. This transience is frustrating. But those moments of happiness are part of what makes life worth living. They arrive, unexpectedly, in many different ways. Sporting success is one kind of elation. But we can also find it through love, friendship, children, memories, play, reading, nature, intellectual enquiry and so much more.

A man with your talents has a lot to give – and a lot to live for. You are still Clarke Carlisle, even though you've stopped playing football. And I hope you'll go on being Clarke Carlisle for many years to come.

Happiness

'. . . but the occasional episode in a general drama
    of pain' – Thomas Hardy

Cloudless skies, old roses coming into flower,
a breeze flicking through The Mayor of Casterbridge.

Toasted granary bread with damson jam,
a pair of goldfinches on the bird feeder.

The whiff of fennel and rosemary,
the farmer's quad bike leaving the field.

Two deckchairs in the shade of a weeping birch.
Everyone you love still alive, last time you heard.

'Happiness' taken from *Shingle Street*, published by Chatto &
Windus, 2015

22. Nicci French

Nicci French is the pseudonym for the writing partnership of journalists Nicci Gerrard and Sean French, who together have written twelve bestselling novels including *The Memory Game*, *Killing Me Softly* and *What To Do When Someone Dies*. The couple are married and live in Suffolk.

Dear Stranger,

You don't know us, and we don't know you. But here is an ordinary sort of story that we wrote for you.

Joe had an old car and it wasn't working. He phoned up Dave and asked if he could help. Dave said, what about Sarah, their old college friend? She had done engineering. Wasn't she good at fixing things?

So on the Saturday morning, they met up in Joe's front yard. Sarah brought her tools because she thought, rightly, that Joe wouldn't have proper ones.

It turned out to be harder than they expected. At first they couldn't even agree on what was wrong. There were even a few bad-tempered moments. When Dave was underneath the car, he got some oil on his new shirt and Joe said it wasn't exactly the right thing to wear for repair work and Dave gave him quite a scary look. A bit later Sarah wondered aloud whether it wouldn't just be better scrapping the car and Joe went very silent.

But after a time they thought they might have found what was wrong. With a bit of effort they managed to extract the part that was the problem. Joe asked if they made them any more. Dave wondered if this might be a job for a garage. Sarah thought for a moment and said, no, they could bypass it. It was a bit fiddly but it might work. They drew a couple of diagrams in pencil on an old bit of paper and found a way they all agreed on.

Joe asked if they wanted some lunch but Sarah said they'd be finished soon. They weren't. To do the bypass, they had to remove some other bits of the engine, and soon there was an alarming array next to the car.

'You do know how to put this back together?' Joe asked nervously.

There were bits of the operation that took all six hands, lining tubes up, tightening bolts. It was almost four o'clock when they all stepped nervously back and looked at their handiwork.

'Well, it *looks* like an engine,' said Dave.

Dubiously, Joe put the key in the ignition and tried it. It started. He got out, shaking his head in disbelief. He went into the house and came back out with three bottles of beer and a half-empty packet of crisps. The three of them sat on the ground looking at the car which was still chugging quietly away. They couldn't bear to switch it off. Sarah shook her head.

'I still think you should scrap it,' she said.

Later, each of them would look on this as the happiest day they had ever spent together.

Happiness isn't a thing. It's not something we can aim for. It's more like heat, the product of a process.

Depression is a thing. Unhappiness is a thing. It is something to be dealt with in all sorts of very different ways.

We shouldn't aim for happiness. We can aim to be busy, to be useful, to challenge ourselves, to be kind, to be in the world, to be with people, with friends. And sometimes, in moments, maybe with a warm beer and half a packet of crisps you'll realise: I was happy.

23. Jo Elworthy

Dr Jo Elworthy is in charge of public education at the Eden Project. She has written many gardening and environment books for adults and children and previously worked as a TV producer and lecturer. She lives in Cornwall with her family.

Dear Stranger,

Do you like soup? Would you mind if I shared a few thoughts with you while I slurp mine? It's the last bowl this year, full of flavours and feelings as well as leeks and potatoes. My mother used to ply me with soup when I was ill or feeling down and I gave, and still give, it to my family for the same reason. The giving as well as the taste helps make things better.

It's frosty outside. The ground heaves as water turns to ice and stretches the soil, opening its pores so it can take deep, cold breaths. In contrast the soup tastes of the warmth of late summer when the ground was warm and crumbly and we lifted pink, pearl-like potatoes from the earth. It tastes of the happy memory of the harvester. It tastes of a wet winter's day as its leeks were pulled like corks from bottles – with a soggy 'pop'. It tastes of the satisfaction of the muddy leaves being peeled back to reveal the white, squeaky stem beneath. The soup is a bowl full of memories of family, friends, sowing, growing, prepping and a sense of happiness in having nurtured the ingredients and then those who have supped it.

My father first showed me the delight of harvesting potatoes. He spent a lot of time in the garden. A hobby, respite from the harder matters in life or immersion in the simple, rewarding things? Whatever the reason, gardening did things for Dad. He's ninety-eight now and still smiles when we discuss the growing season. I've gardened all my life and find it calming and satisfying. It provides space in which to quietly think – or not, sometimes it feels good to just empty the mind. It enables time to just peacefully be – sometimes alone, sometimes with good company. I remember a tricky time between homes when there was no garden. There were soon two pots of soil, some seeds and mint for tea and parsley for the obligatory 'green alive stuff' to enable that 'earthing' feeling.

The flavours in the soup stir further memories of those who have shared their stories. Here are a few spoonfuls.

Darren left school before the exams; he 'couldn't be assed'. He joined our gardening scheme. We had a one-acre walled garden, a broken rotavator, fifteen teenagers (some broken), a polytunnel and a lot of attitude (some good). A year later we had a meal, sown, grown, cooked and served by Darren et al. with a smile and a swagger. Darren's now a landscape gardener, still with the same swagger.

Rosie

We are not alone. Bacterial cells outnumber our own 10:1. These 'communities' that live within and on our bodies are, in the main, essential. They help our immune systems develop, help digest the food in our gut and some of them protect us from the bad bacteria that make us sick. One friendly little one, *Mycobacterium vaccae*, may possibly affect our mood and memory. Some trials have found it reduces anxiety and raises serotonin levels in the brain. It is found in the earth and the air. Gardening may help our wellbeing in more ways than one.

Gabi

We wanted to make a showcase garden to raise some edgy issues and to dig into some of the deeper benefits of gardening. We worked with communities of people who had experienced homelessness, drug abuse, loneliness, difficult times . . . Together we grew plants, mutual respect and self-worth. I was digging planting holes. Fred took my spade. 'Let me.' Not wishing to let the female side down, I said I could manage. 'Let me,' he insisted. 'If I dig I get tired. If I get tired, I don't wake at night.'

I was drawn into a new world. The gardening environment created a bond and a level playing field with a common language. In a year we had grown to five hundred volunteers. Together we designed, planted, made and hosted the biggest garden ever made at the Chelsea Flower Show. The themes: health and wellbeing, the senses, the environment, industry and food. The experience helped people to learn to fly again – many now have jobs, self-respect and hope. Gardening is nurturing. Caring for and showing compassion for living things helps to heal the hurt.

Jane

One of the groups that worked on the garden, Grounded Ecotherapy, went on to work on the roof garden at the Southbank, still going strong for all to see.

To be able to design, build and nurture the garden on the Thames at Southbank Centre with our team is, to this date, one of the biggest challenges of my life. Seven years ago, I was a broken man, both physically and mentally, living on the streets with methadone, heroin and alcohol numbing the misery of life. How I got there is a long story. Today I am clean, employed as a horticulture teacher in our group, Grounded Ecotherapy, paying my own rent for the first time in thirty years. Horticulture has changed my life.

Paul, founder of Grounded Ecotherapy: 'We offer recovery for people and places.'

I've been told that occasionally I'm unpredictable, withdrawn, depressed . . . But there's a bridge between the two worlds I live in – *the light side and the dark side*. This bridge feels like a garden with space and growth. I have learned to recognise the dark side calling and these days I rarely cross the bridge. Instead I stay on it. Whenever I see darkness in others, I invite them to learn the joys that are on the bridge: the joy of watching nature act like an antidepressant, of having time to think and to be able to create without competing. It's a non-judgemental garden. It protects us.

Ken, co-founder of People and Gardens

Does 'the answer lie in the soil' as the old adage goes? Does it lie in a reconnection with nature? Does it lie with family and friendships and caring for, connecting to and understanding each other? Does it lie with a sense of nurturing or a social purpose? More likely it's like the soup: a blend of many things. This bowl is now finished so it's time to sign off. Thanks for letting me share some thoughts with you. Now it's time to go back out into the garden to take some deep breaths and plan where to sow the leeks next year.

With best wishes,
Jo

24. John Lewis-Stempel

John Lewis-Stempel is a writer and farmer. His many previous books include *Meadowland: The Private Life of an English Field*, *The Wild Life: A Year of Living on Wild Food* and the bestselling *Six Weeks: The Short and Gallant Life of the British Officer in the First World War*. He lives on the border of England and Wales with his wife and two children.

Dear You,

They say we don't know each other, but we have met. Every day of our lives. You are me, I am you. Those people on the high street smiling together without an apparent care in the world, separated from you because someone has put a giant glass jar over you? The air-tight one, with the glass six inches thick? Sometimes when they go home, they cradle their head in their hands and think, Oh God.

And don't *you*, even when you are a foetus in the bottom of the well, crawl up, stand up and assume the brave face? (Usually for the sake of others.) Loneliness, unhappiness . . . occur with us all. It's a part of who we all are.

The Black Dog is on me today. Jumping up, paws on my shoulder, teeth bright-sharp, tongue hanging out.

But wagging her tail. Madly. Irrepressibly. Happily.

Her name is Edith, and she is my black Labrador. (Actually, her name is Eadgifu Swanneshals, aka Edith Swan-neck; I was going through a serious Anglo-Saxon phase when I got her.) Churchill was ace in standing up to Hitler, yet was way off the bull's eye in characterising depression as a 'Black Dog'. Because Edith – and she is representing dog-kind here – is infallibly able to wring a smile and make me un-lonely. She doesn't give a Labrador fart if I've got rampant eczema on my face or if I'm fuck useless at everything. She never judges. Her default is pure, distilled, one hundred percent proof enthusiasm for life. She is a tug-boat and sometimes all I have to do is hold on to her lead. She is written through from nose to tail with loyalty, and she really likes to be with me. Even when I'm wrong. Especially when I'm wrong.

I'm not being trite or naive here. There are real anthropological, physiological reasons why dogs can guide the hurting, as well as the deaf and the blind. Dogs produce all the right '-orphins' and '-amines' in us. Dogs, anthropologists tell us, were the first animal domesticated by man. Or, as the Israeli historian Yuval Harari has it, tongue only very slightly in cheek, *Homo sapiens* became domesticated by dogs, since breeding wild-eyed wolves into kindly eyed fidos required humankind to associate and communicate. Whatever. Dogs and us have history – about 15,000 years of it, to be more or less exact. In that vast time dogs have learned a trick or two about looking after humans.

So, I just wanted to say: you are never lonely if you have a dog.

It's just a thought.

As ever, with all best wishes,
John Lewis-Stempel

25. Chris Riddell

Chris Riddell is an acclaimed artist of children's books and a political cartoonist for the *Observer*. Amongst other titles, Chris illustrates the *Ottoline* young fiction series and the *Goth Girl* series, as well as working closely with Paul Stewart on the *Edge Chronicles* and *Wyrmeweald*. He has won many awards for his work, including the Nestlé Gold Award, the UNESCO Award for *Something Else* and the rare honour of two Kate Greenaway Medals.

26. Tessa Watt

Tessa Watt is an experienced mindfulness teacher and consultant. She is co-presenter of the Mental Health Foundation's online mindfulness course and part of a team supporting the All-party Parliamentary Group for Mindfulness at Westminster. In her earlier career she was a senior producer with BBC Radio and Music. Her books include *Introducing Mindfulness* and *Mindful London*. Tessa lives in London with her family.

You don't know me, but they say we're all interconnected, so maybe we've crossed paths some time in our travels. Maybe we sat next to each other on a train, negotiating space for our elbows and packages. Or maybe you've seen me on Facebook, linking arms with a mutual friend of a friend, smiling to freeze the happiness of the moment for all time. Or perhaps you were the one smiling on Facebook, while I sat at my computer looking at photos of the happy occasion. That's what we're all doing on Facebook, isn't it? Showing ourselves and the world how happy we are, how happy our lives are?

I have a confession: I am not a person with a special talent for happiness. In fact, for the first decades of my life, I would say I was pretty clever at being dissatisfied. Not so much with the big things, like my career, which seemed to be going well, but the little things, the moment-by-moment experiences. I found it hard to settle wherever I was without worrying that things were a bit better somewhere else. If I had a choice of two things to do in an evening, I'd spend my time feeling anxious at having made the wrong choice. Standing in front of a buffet with five desserts, I'd have to have a little of all of them. Perhaps more importantly, I was often dissatisfied with my inner life: while it might seem like I had the right ingredients for happiness, often my emotions were anxious or jealous or unhappy.

Around my thirtieth birthday, I discovered meditation. I also heard about what the Buddhists call 'the truth of suffering'. It might sound pessimistic, but it came to me as a big relief. From this perspective, suffering is an inescapable part of being human. 'Suffering' includes the big things: illness, a broken heart, losing our job, bereavement, the realisation that we don't live for ever. But it also includes the low-level dissatisfaction of daily life, the constant sense of things being not quite right. We may spend our lives trying to set up perfect moments which fail to live up to our expectations. Coming home from work, we dream of a hot bath with a cold glass of wine . . . but the bath isn't hot enough, the wine isn't cold enough. Even if we get things just right, they don't stay that way – the phone rings and we have to jump out, dripping water over the floor. On the bigger scale, if we do get our job or our relationship just where we want it to be, we can hardly enjoy it for fear that at any moment things will change. When we look clearly, we see that nothing in life is frozen, except perhaps in those grinning pictures on Facebook.

Meditation doesn't fix things and make everything perfect. It is based on an approach to happiness which is paradoxically not about trying to be happy. In fact, it's based on the idea that it's OK NOT to be happy. We can be OK with being sad, angry, wound up with adrenalin or flat with boredom. Human experience is much more interesting than being happy all the time. Do we really want only Pharrell Williams singing 'Happy' twenty-four hours a day? Or do we also want Adele's heartbreak, Wagner's drama, Ed Sheeran's sadness and the Rolling Stones' dissatisfaction?

Meditation is a practice in learning how to be with our experience just as it is in this moment, including every tone and timbre and nuance of human emotion. And what this brings may not be 'happiness' as such, but a kind of contentment that things are OK as they are. It's even OK to be 'not OK'. We could call it equanimity: not that we don't feel strongly about things, but that at the deepest level we are fine just as we are.

Meditation – or 'mindfulness' as we call the secular version – has become a buzzword, and if you're like me you may feel resistant to things that are hyped by the media. But when the buzz dies down, its popularity will continue to grow, because this movement is spread by word of mouth, by people who've discovered it for themselves. We take it for granted that we look after our bodies with exercise, but we're beginning to realise that we also need to look after our minds.

Mindfulness is a training in how to be present, using a simple focus like our breath. You could try it right now if you like. You could take a wakeful sitting posture, feeling your feet on the ground and the weight of your bottom on the seat. Then begin to notice that you are breathing. You don't have to change your breath, just bring awareness to some place in the body where you feel it. It could be the nostrils, belly, chest, or some sense of flow. Each time your mind wanders off, this is not because you're a bad meditator; this is what the mind naturally does. When you notice your attention has gone somewhere else, see if you can let go of whatever took it away, and gently escort it back to the breath. Over and over again. Slowly you are retraining the mind to be willing to be with what is here right now: this breath, this moment, as it is.

You can get a sense of the basics of mindfulness meditation using apps and books, and to go deeper, the best way is to learn from an experienced teacher. For me, meditation is now woven into the fabric of my life – something I practise every day, and which permeates my way of being. After twenty years I'm not sure if I can say I'm 'happy', but I'm more content, less dissatisfied. I can pick one dessert and savour it without eyeing up the others. I can enjoy a holiday without spending the whole time caught in worries. I can feel sadness without keeping busy to avoid it. I can spend time by myself and be content with my own company. I can appreciate the vividness of the little experiences which make up my life – the sunshine coming through the window, the hot cup of tea in my hands, the aching melody of a song, a conversation with a friend. Is this happiness? I think it'll do for me. What do you think, dear stranger?

27. Helen Dunmore

Helen Dunmore is a novelist, poet, short story and children's writer. She has published thirteen novels, of which the most recent is *The Lie*, shortlisted for the Walter Scott Prize for Historical Fiction. She was the inaugural winner of the Orange Prize for Fiction for *A Spell of Winter*. Her work is translated into more than thirty languages and she is a Fellow of the Royal Society of Literature.

A Letter to the Secretary of State for Health

Dear Secretary of State,

The election is over, your party is now in government, and you have just returned from Downing Street. The job you have wanted for years is yours. Who knows how you feel this morning? Proud, perhaps, or elated, or determined. You may be apprehensive about the responsibility. You may even be happy.

What does the future hold for you? You will be stressed, certainly. You will be criticised, and high office won't protect you from humiliation if your party decides that you are a liability. You may even lose your job, and find that suddenly you are one of us again, without a driver to take you wherever you need to go. You will no longer have aides to smooth your path and feed your sense of your own significance. Instead, you may lie awake at night, going over and over what you did and what you failed to do.

I'm sorry to dwell on such things when for you this is a bright, confident morning. What I want to ask you to do is to use your imagination, every day that you are in government, and to remember that patients are not other people: they are you.

You have the ultimate responsibility for the running of the National Health Service. As we have been told so many times, to govern is to make choices. For far too long, successive governments have chosen to push mental health to the back of the queue when it comes

to funding, as if the pain of those who have
depression or schizophrenia were not as significant or
worthy of treatment as the pain of those who have
cancer or heart disease. If you look about you, the
results of this choice are everywhere. The NHS
estimates that ninety percent of people who attempt
suicide or die by suicide have one or more mental
conditions. The suicide rate in the UK is disturbingly
high, and it is climbing. If any other illness were
causing so much death among young people, it would
be an urgent priority for funding.

People lose their jobs and drop out of education
because they have a mental illness and are not
receiving adequate treatment. There are long waiting
lists for therapy, even though research shows, for
example, that anti-depressants are most effective
when combined with therapy. There are GPs who need
further training so that they fully understand the
action of the drugs they are prescribing. There is a
shortage of psychiatrists and therapists. There are
helplines which need money, and there are people
who need a safe place in which to recover.

Perhaps you do not need to imagine any of this. It is
quite possible that you belong to the one in four who
has a mental illness at some stage of life. If you do, I
hope that you are one of the lucky ones. I hope you
receive the best possible treatment, as soon as you
need it. I hope you do not have to wait for weeks for a
telephone assessment, or experience frightening
side-effects from your drugs and struggle to get the
information you want. If you are part of the one in
four, you know what it is like not to feel safe in your
own mind. You know that for other people to talk to
you about happiness is completely beside the point.
You have a long journey to make before that word
will begin to seem relevant to you, and what you need
are people who will be at your side, offering the best
of what mental health care can provide.

I am old enough to remember a time when cancer was an illness that no one talked about. There were few successful treatments, and there was stigma. To us now, that seems shocking. Perhaps, in thirty or forty years' time, people will look back in amazement at the stigmatisation of mental illnesses. They will be shocked at how primitive our treatments were in the second decade of the twenty-first century. And perhaps they will point to you as one of the politicians who pushed for research money, who expanded treatment programmes, who was determined that mental health should never again be shoved into second place.

I wish you well in your new job.

Yours sincerely,
Helen Dunmore

28. Alain de Botton

Alain de Botton's bestselling books include *Religion for Atheists*, *How Proust Can Change Your Life*, *The Art of Travel*, *The Pleasures and Sorrows of Work* and *The Architecture of Happiness*. He lives in London and founded The School of Life (www.theschooloflife.com) and Living Architecture (www.living-architecture.co.uk). For more information, consult www.alaindebotton.com.

On Calm

Nowadays, almost all of us wish we could be calmer. It's one of the distinctive longings of the modern age. Across history, people have tended to seek out adventure and excitement. But most of us have had a bit too much of that now. The desire to be more tranquil and focused is the new, ever more urgent priority.

In our view, there are eight basic causes of agitation – and the path to greater calm involves attempting to consider each one systematically and returning to it on a regular basis. Here is the start of a three-part guide to a calmer life:

One: Panic about panic

A lot of agitation is caused by an unrealistic sense of how unusual difficulty is. We are oppressed by unhelpful images of how easy it is to achieve and how normal it is to succeed. The stories that officially circulate about what relationships and careers are like tend fatally to downplay the darker realities, leaving many of us not only upset, but upset that we are upset, feeling persecuted as well as miserable.

If your life is rather more difficult than this saccharine image, it must be that you are a freak or a failure.

We need to change our points of reference about what life is like. We need – in the broadest sense – better art, a

kind that takes us more truthfully into the realities of relationships, the workplace and our 3 a.m. panics. We need to
make sure we are surrounded by accurate case studies of
the ordinary miseries of daily life.

The agony in the kitchen

Consider this example of the life of a couple. Many things
are going well for them. Earlier, one of their children showed
them such a sweet drawing she'd done at school. They had a
nice holiday last year. They love playing soccer together in
the park (the mum gets really competitive and has discovered she's a brilliant goalkeeper). They are trying to work
out whether to move to a village outside the city. Sometimes they feel so close. But this evening is a nightmare.
She received a flirtatious email from an ex-boyfriend of
years ago; she hasn't shown it to her husband, but it's on
her mind as a source of torment. It's opened up imaginative
possibilities. She has put her head in her hands – but he's
said twenty times that drives him nuts. His mother used to
do that. Their marriage is OK. They've been together nine
years. They're going to survive long term but, right now,
they're about to have a titanic fight. He'll call her a bitch
and slam the door, but he's quite nice – genuinely . . .

We should contemplate this situation to reduce panic
about our relationships. Difficulty is normal. Very decent
couples have long-running and extraordinarily vicious conflicts over apparently small things. In a good relationship,
two nights out of five you will wonder what you are doing
together. That is success. It's worth repeating: two bad
nights a week is lucky.

The French eighteenth-century philosopher Chamfort
wisely observed: 'A person should swallow a toad every
morning to be sure of not meeting with anything more
revolting in the day ahead.' Disgusting things are on the

menu for all of us. Life, it seems, is – in many ways – about quite a lot of suffering.

Christianity is upfront about the idea that our lives will be burdened by suffering. You don't have to believe in the religion (we don't) to recognise there's something important at play here. Christianity takes the view that loss, self-reproach, failure, regret, sickness and sadness will always find ways of entering life. Our troubles need practical help, of course. But Christianity identifies another need as well: for our suffering to be recognised as normal.

The Crucifixion universalises suffering. A good – indeed perfect – man was humiliated, injured and ultimately killed. This invites us to contemplate the centrality of suffering in the achievement of all valuable goals. Rather than concentrate on the moment of fulfilment – when one feels the joy of success – we must direct our attention to the times of hardship and sacrifice and consider that they are the most important, the most deserving of admiration.

Such dark notions strengthen us a little – and offer valuable consolation – for the hard tasks of our lives.

Two: Taking too much responsibility

We over-personalise our fates, taking too much credit in the good times, and then, too much blame in the bad ones. It's tempting to take all the credit when there is a triumph. But the corollary is that we are entirely to blame when we are humiliated and beaten.

We are particularly prone to over-personalisation when it comes to money. To keep our agitation in check, we should embrace an economic perspective that allows us to see ourselves as operating within a huge system loosely designated as 'Capitalism'. Regular contemplation of the New York

Stock Exchange reminds us that the way the world works is not our own doing. Powerful forces sweep over whole industries, condemning some to decline, while raising others to remarkable (if unstable) prosperity. The key point is: much about your fate is not your own work. You did not invent the world. You are not personally entirely responsible for your condition. The suffering is real, but remember that it is less personal than we tend to suppose.

Consider now the Roman goddess of fortune. The Romans knew her as 'Fortuna'. She was to be found on the back of most Roman coins, holding a cornucopia in one hand and a rudder in the other. She was beautiful and usually wore a light tunic and smiled attractively. The cornucopia was a symbol of her power to bestow favours, but the rudder was a symbol of her more sinister power to change destinies, just like that. She could scatter gifts (a love affair, a great job, beautiful children), then with terrifying speed shift the rudder's course, maintaining a chilling smile as she watched us choke to death on a fishbone, disappear in a landslide or go bankrupt in a credit crisis.

The goddess of fortune remains useful to keep our exposure to accident, luck and fate continually in our minds; she conflates a range of threats to our security into one ghastly anthropomorphic enemy.

Not everything that happens to us occurs with reference to something about us. Our romantic or professional failure does not have to be read as retribution for some sin we have committed, it is not always rational punishment handed out after careful examination of all the evidence by an all-seeing Providence in a divine courtroom; it may be a cruel, but morally meaningless, by-product of the machinations of a rancorous goddess. The interventions of fortune, of 'luck', whether they are kindly or diabolical, introduce a random element into human destiny.

To be calm, we must reduce the weight of our proud and unrealistic modern individualism.

Three: Being too hopeful
A major source of agitation is, strange as it might at first sound, optimism. The expectation that things will go well creates anxiety because, at some level, we know that we can't quite count on our hopes coming to fruition. And of course, as things turn out, quite often they don't. We are on tenterhooks – and we suffer.

To restore calm we need to become strategically pessimistic. That is, to spend more time getting used to the very real possibility that things will work out rather badly. A lot of good projects fail, most things go wrong, at least half our dreams won't work out. Pessimism dampens unhelpful and impatient expectations.

It is hope – with regard to our careers, our love lives, our children, our politicians and our planet – that is primarily to blame for angering and embittering us. The incompatibility between the scale of our aspirations and the reality of life generates the anxious disappointments which spoil so many days.

There are some extremely helpful pessimists in the history of philosophy, waiting to cheer us up. The French philosopher Blaise Pascal stands out for the exceptionally therapeutic nature of his gloom. In his book, the *Pensées*, Pascal misses no opportunities to confront his readers with evidence of how badly things normally turn out. In seductive classical French, he informs us that happiness is an illusion ('Anyone who does not see the vanity of the world is very vain himself'), that misery is the norm ('If our condition were truly happy we should not need to divert ourselves from thinking about it') and that we have to face the desperate facts of our situation head on: 'Man's greatness comes from knowing he is wretched'.

Given the tone, it comes as something of a surprise to discover that reading Pascal is not at all the depressing experience one might have presumed. The work is consoling, heart-warming and even, at times, hilarious. For those teetering on the verge of despair, there can paradoxically be no finer book to turn to than one which seeks to grind man's every last hope into the dust. As a result, the *Pensées* is far more cheering than any sentimental volume touting inner beauty, positive thinking or the realisation of hidden potential.

There is relief, which can explode into bursts of laughter, when we finally come across evidence that our very worst insights, far from being unique and shameful, are part of the common, inevitable reality of mankind. Our dread that we might be the only ones to feel anxious, bored, jealous, cruel, perverse and narcissistic turns out to be gloriously unfounded, opening up unexpected opportunities for communion around our dark realities.

We should honour Pascal, and the long line of pessimistic philosophers to which he belongs, for doing us the incalculably great favour of publicly and elegantly rehearsing the facts of life.

This is not a stance with which the modern world betrays much sympathy, for one of its dominant characteristics, and certainly its greatest flaw, is its optimism.

Despite occasional moments of panic, most often connected to market crises, wars or pandemics, the secular age maintains an all but irrational devotion to a narrative of improvement, based on a messianic faith in the three great drivers of change: science, technology and business. Material improvements since the mid-eighteenth century have been so remarkable, and have so exponentially increased our comfort, safety, wealth and power, as to deal an almost fatal blow to our capacity to remain pessimistic – and therefore, crucially, to our ability to stay calm. It has been impossible to hold on to a balanced assessment of what life is likely to provide for us when we have witnessed the cracking of the genetic code, the invention of the mobile phone, the opening of Western-style supermarkets in remote corners of China and the launch of the Hubble telescope.

Yet while it is undeniable that the scientific and economic trajectories of mankind have been pointed firmly in an upward direction for several centuries, we do not comprise mankind: none of us individuals can dwell exclusively amidst the ground-breaking developments in genetics or telecommunications that lend our age its distinctive and buoyant prejudices. We may derive some benefit from the availability of hot baths and computer chips, but our lives are no less subject to accident, frustrated ambition, heartbreak, jealousy, anxiety or death than were those of our medieval forebears. But at least our ancestors had the advantage of living in pessimistic times which never made the mistake of promising its population that happiness could ever make a permanent home for itself on this earth.

It's worth adding that a pessimistic worldview does not have to entail a life stripped of joy. Pessimists can have a far greater capacity for appreciation than optimists, for they never expect things to turn out well and so may be amazed by the modest successes which occasionally break across their darkened horizons. It's quite possible to be both pessimistic and, day to day, a real laugh.

29. Deborah Levy

Deborah Levy is a novelist and playwright. Her novels include the acclaimed *Swimming Home* (shortlisted for the Man Booker Prize), *Billy and Girl*, *The Unloved*, *Beautiful Mutants* and *Swallowing Geography*. Her short story collection, *Black Vodka*, was shortlisted for the International Frank O'Connor Award. Deborah's autobiographical essay on writing, *Things I Don't Want To Know*, is published by Penguin and she is currently writing the sequel. Her new novel, *Hot Milk*, will be published in 2016.

Dear Stranger,

I have begun this letter a few times now but so far I haven't believed what I'm writing. I am a novelist and have written books on the subject of happiness and how there is so much pressure on us all to be happy that it can start to feel like we are calmly unhappy and everyone else is hysterically happy. But it doesn't feel right to find random extracts from my books to share with you here, so I am going to start with something that is happening in my own life.

As I write this letter, my elderly mother is perhaps fatally unwell in hospital.

I have to be careful because if she becomes well enough to read this, maybe I will feel totally shy and foolish. She is not a stranger after all, though at the moment, I don't think my mother currently feels like herself, as the saying goes.

I have found a few ways of coping.

It's a long walk to get to her ward. I walk down the corridors very fast like a soldier. I tell myself that if I slow down I might just turn around and run away. And I have made a rule that I will always look very smart when I visit my mother. So I take time putting on clothes I like wearing and doing my hair and it makes me laugh because I look like I'm going to an important meeting with a lot at stake. But this is an important meeting and there is a lot at stake.

Yesterday I was wearing a red dress and boots and did the usual soldier walk to the ward, clip-clop-clop-clip (I can see why armies practise the art of marching – it resembles a steady heartbeat even if we are scared and our hearts are going berserk) and then when I enter the ward, I change the metabolism of that pace, walk softly, slowly.

I always sit on my mother's bed rather than on the bulky visitor's chair which is arranged at some distance with a table between us. No matter how unwell she is, I always say to her, 'move up', and though it is physically painful (tubes attached to her) she does, she makes a space for me. It is the most subtle of movements. The human endeavour it has taken to make that space is immense. Sometimes it's just two centimetres, but to me it is as vast as a night sky crowded with stars.

I bought her a radio and some headphones and started to put them together. The earpieces were massive, the size of two small black kittens. I placed them on the skull of her head while I tuned the radio to a programme I thought she would like. While she listened I perched in the space she had made for me and put some moisturiser on her lips, which get dry in hospital. Now and again she lifted her hand to touch the red material of my dress. After a while she said, 'Crows have brains that are as big as a gorilla's. They can recognise people, they have a memory.'

I knew this information was from the programme she was listening to. I was pleased she was surprised. I didn't know that about crows either. After a while I left her to take my teenage daughter out for her favourite lunch – jerk chicken with rice and peas. Jerk, in case you don't know, is a spicy sauce from Jamaica and the chicken is marinated in it. That was Sunday. It wasn't the best or the worst day. This is not a life-affirming letter; it's just about a few moments in a bad situation.

I don't have a moral position on happiness. We have to find our own point to life, even if it's to learn something new about crows. I guess that's an existential position, isn't it?

Talking of uncomfortable positions, I remember someone telling me how he actually lay under his dying mother's bed in the hospital when visiting hours were over. The lights were out and every now and again he popped his head round to whisper, 'Hello'. That was an inspired, eccentric idea. Here's a quote from Proust about the worth of ideas:

Griefs, at the moment when they change into ideas, lose some of their power to injure our heart.

It would be true to say this quote has been lying under my bed for all of my life.

Thank you for your attention, distinguished stranger,
Deborah

Dedicated to my beloved mother, Philippa Beatrice Murrell, who died a month after this was written.

30. Kevin Bridges

Kevin Bridges, Scotland's 'young comedy prodigy' (*Guardian*), has followed a meteoric path, from his first five-minute set in The Stand comedy club in Glasgow to selling out the SECC to a record-breaking 100,000 fans. At the tender age of just twenty-seven, Kevin has recently put pen to paper to tell his story in his brilliant memoir, *We Need to Talk About . . . Kevin Bridges*. Born in Clydebank, he still lives in Glasgow.

It's Monday morning and today I have two letters to write; one to you and one to pay-per-view TV channel Premier Sports.

I had initially contacted the good people at Premier Sports by telephone immediately after the pre-season friendly tournament in which my football team were playing and which Premier Sports had the broadcasting rights for, with regards to terminating my £7.99 monthly subscription, only to be told they operate a more intimate and personable customer cancellation policy and that written correspondence was my only hope of an escape.

It's taken me a while to get round to writing them a letter, even though I haven't watched the channel long enough for the programme information bar to disappear from the screen since that July afternoon when my team's fringe players managed a 1–1 draw with a German lower league side.

Today is the day though, the day I let them know that it's over, that we're going our separate ways.

That's for this afternoon though, maybe even tomorrow or another month. Maybe I'll stay. Who knows?

First of all though, I'd like to say hello to you. I don't know who you are and you may or may not know who I am. I won't be offended if you don't know me but I'd imagine I'd feel a short, intense hit of relevance if you did. I'd feel validated and that would leave me wanting more, wanting to know if you were a fan of me, what jokes of mine were your favourites...
and so on.

Feelings of insecurity, low self-esteem and a yearning for reassurance are things that are synonymous with comedians, to the point that I felt reluctant to ever seek any help with my moods and general state of mind, for the fear of being labelled as another clichéd sad clown.

I'd pictured a doctor or a therapist dismissively asking me what I had to feel down about, quickly rattling off a list of the positives in my life, a list that I'd imagine anyone who I told about how I felt would quickly run through before countering my problems with a list of *real* problems, making me feel ashamed, guilty, embarrassed and worse, much worse.

I'd have a voice somewhere in my head agreeing, my internal commentator, the one that would cynically analyse every word I said, every thought I thought, every move, every action.

I knew that I had a great life, potentially, so what the fuck was my problem? Why did I feel isolated, lonely and constantly anxious, why had I lost all interest in the World around me. I didn't know how to talk about it. I watched all the documentaries on depression and read so many articles but it still didn't make sense to me. I couldn't fathom how someone could be sad without being able to pinpoint exactly why.

I didn't know how to tell anyone about my thoughts and how I'd stopped feeling any emotions other than ones of despondency where everything left me underwhelmed. I'd only feel feelings of relief when I'd go to bed at night, as though I was grateful that another day was over. I'd set my alarm hours before I had to wake up, to delay the start of the next day, to prepare myself for having to leave the house and get through it all again.

I could talk to those close to me about how worthless I felt but I was reluctant to go into the full details for fear of alarming them and creating more problems. For this reason, I preferred to be away from those I loved, to be alone, a burden to no one except myself.

I wasn't able to concentrate on anything to take my mind off my mood. I couldn't read, watch movies, watch football, listen to music, nothing. I struggled to function at work and I felt myself spiralling.

I had stopped drinking alcohol so I didn't have the option of blocking it all out, thankfully. I'd tried this before and it only delayed the misery and brought along its own set of problems, ensuring the dark moods returned even stronger, a rollover.

I realised that I'd exhausted everyone around me and that I couldn't continue self-destructing. I decided to challenge my preconceived ideas of what a visit to a doctor with a mental problem rather than a physical problem would be like. Thankfully, I'd gone over on my ankle playing five-aside football a week before and I was still struggling to walk so I figured that could be my back-up plan if I crumbled, if my bottle crashed, if the voice in my head was laughing at me, asking me who I thought I was. 'Tony Soprano?' At least with my ankle ligament damage, I had something tangible to justify the appointment.

I sat in my GP's waiting room; the waiting room I'd known since childhood but this was by far the most important visit I'd ever made. I looked around at the posters on the wall, one in particular, encouraging people with symptoms of depression, stress and anxiety to come forward, to speak to someone, to get help.

I knew I was hardly unique, that so many people have felt or are feeling the way I felt, especially in today's World, with all the pressures we put on ourselves, our constant comparisons of our own lives to those around us, to those of the people we don't even know but who we have as friends on social media. 500 friends? Who the fuck has 500 friends?

I got through the doctor's appointment without even a mention of my football injury, which would have made for a far more masculine visit to the doctor. 'I've done my ankle in, playing five-aside with the lads' I could have proudly announced, slumped on his chair, untying my new Nike trainer to proudly display the swelling. 'I still played on, though.'

I was given a list of cognitive behaviour therapists in my area, I limped my way out of the health centre and immediately phoned up one of the numbers and booked myself an appointment.

Speaking to a therapist felt like something I should have done years ago, it allowed me to talk, openly, honestly and without the feeling that I was giving someone else my problems and dragging them down with me. I was speaking to someone with no prejudice, no emotional attachment to me, a professional, someone who understood how the brain works, the same way a physiotherapist understands how ankle ligaments and tendons work.

To cut to the point here, I found it unbelievably liberating to talk through every thought I'd had, everything that had been weighing me down and leaving me pinned to my bed, hiding from the World.

I was asked simply, 'How are you?'

As casual and disarming as that and that was it, I'd done the hardest part. I was speaking to someone. I couldn't stop speaking.

The voice in my head disappeared as soon as I'd mentioned it, like I'd grassed on him and he'd immediately fled the scene.

As I spoke about my problems out loud I began to realise how irrational most of them were – some rational – not everything weighing me down was a creation of my own mind but even those problems, I was able to hear someone else's take on them which helped me work up the skills and a new approach to coping with them.

I was asked to re-consider my daily routine, to address the bad habits I'd slipped into which I acknowledged were both a consequence of my mental state and a contributing factor.

It took me time and a lot of effort to get used to a new lifestyle and a new outlook, to surrender control over life's inevitabilities, to stop fixating on the past and fretting about the future from the limited vantage point of the present.

Like a lot of people, I wasn't taking time to live in the moment, to live in the centre of myself rather than hiding somewhere in the back of my mind, daydreaming, letting so much pass me by. I'd lost focus of what truly made me happy and who truly made me happy.

I put some new habits into place, realising that I'd have to work a little harder in order to break out of this horrible rut and halt the descent, common sense stuff like exercising, eating better, spending less time on the Internet, freeing up the space in my head to think and form an understanding of myself and an understanding of others, reading more, finding new interests, speaking to people, asking more questions and, of course, re-watching old episodes of *The Simpsons*.

On my third therapy session, I told of how the day before I'd been swimming, got back to work, back to enjoying work, caught up with my mum and dad and cooked a healthy meal for myself and how happy all of this had made me.

I panicked because it had made me not just happy, but elated, to the point that I didn't know what was happening. I felt like I wanted to run out into the street, singing, like an actor in a Broadway musical, grabbing someone and cuddling them. I felt myself fill with tears and realised I had to rein myself in a bit. It was a release of so much pressure, anxiety, the demons being forcibly ejected out of my head.

I laughed as I re-told the story of this out-of-body experience and the therapist laughed too.

She concluded that this was normal and that this feeling of genuine happiness had placed me out of my comfort zone. I hadn't been this happy in a while.

Although I've never quite felt an overwhelming happiness like that since – I'd imagine I'd need some pretty powerful stimulants to recreate that level of euphoria – I felt more content, more relaxed and I've learned not to panic when I feel myself go in a bad mood.

A lot of stuff pisses me off and I have my faults, failings and things about myself I dislike, but don't we all? It's what connects us.

We're all fighting the same battle; I believe we all have doubts about ourselves, about our place in the World, about our purpose and what we have to offer.

Maybe the new iPhone 6 will make you happy, but then the iPhone 7 will come out and you'll be unhappy. Maybe alcohol or drugs will make you happy but then they'll wear off and how will that leave you?

Maybe seeing a dog leaning out of a car window with its tongue hanging out and its ears flapping in the wind will make you happy, who knows, it's entirely up to you.

I'm not an expert on happiness, far from it, and this letter I'm sending to you, a stranger, has no basis more reliable than my own meandering experience, to quote Baz Luhrmann from the opening of the Sunscreen Song.

You're the first person I've told all of this to so there we are; I hope you don't feel like a stranger. I hope you never do.

If you feel low, talk to someone; know that you're not alone and that there is potentially something beautiful at the other end.

I feel glad that we spoke; so glad that I think I'll remain a Premier Sports customer, for at least another day anyway.

I hope this letter finds you in good health (I think you're supposed to say that at the start of a letter, fuck knows. As I said, I'm not the most prolific of letter writers).

Yours sincerely (There, that's a bit more like it!),
Kevin Bridges

31. Marian Keyes

Marian Keyes is one of the most successful Irish novelists of all time. Her internationally bestselling novels, including *Rachel's Holiday*, *Anybody Out There* and *The Brightest Star in the Sky*, deal variously with modern ailments, including addiction, depression, domestic violence, the glass ceiling and serious illness, and are always written with compassion, humour and hope. In 2009, Marian experienced the start of a major depressive episode, and had to stop any work. Eventually she found that baking cakes helped her survive; and in 2012, she published *Saved by Cake*, which combines recipes with autobiography. Marian lives in Dublin with her husband.

From childhood we're fed fairy stories of princesses waking from a deep sleep when her prince kisses her, or of a glass slipper fitting perfectly, indicating that this is definitely true love. So it's hardly our fault that we think there's one perfect man out there for us and if we wait long enough, he'll eventually show up and say, 'Hello there, I'm your The One! Let's buy a flat together and sand the floors!'

I internalised this message so deeply that at the age of *six* I was worried that no one would marry me, and I formulated a secret fall-back plan where, if no candidate stepped forward, I could marry my brother.

I spent my twenties doing anxious, eagle-eyed scans of every man I met, wondering Are you The One? Are you The One? I *hated* not having a boyfriend – judge me all you like, I'm just being honest – and I often woke at 4 a.m., consumed with fear that I would always be alone.

Whenever I met a man who could possibly be The One, I jumped straight into things, ready to commence my shiny, perfect life. Right! Let's get this show on the road!

Sometimes I had boyfriends who were nice, decent men but I always got bored. Then I met someone who was probably a nice, decent man also but was deeply unsuitable for me, so there was a lot of jealousy and door-slamming and 'Stop the car, I'm getting out here!' There were break-ups and make-ups and because I was so consumed with the drama of it all, I was CERTAIN that he was The One. But he wasn't – I was simply addicted to the adrenalin.

And then I met the man I eventually married. As luck would have it, I'd had a spell in rehab and had learned some 'important things' — for example, if I let a man (or anyone) make me feel bad about myself, things probably weren't right.

Himself was different from any of the other boyfriends I had because we were friends for a good while before anything happened. I fancied him madly (twenty years on, I still do) but I made myself wait. Meanwhile, he rang when he said he would and picked me up at the arranged time and in the past, I'd have scorned such behaviour, but now I appreciated it. Then there were all kinds of things that I didn't even notice at the time, but were actually very important: we shared common values, we were both a bit lefty. There were other resonances — both our dads were accountants and we were almost the same age and shared the same cultural references; also we both had a dodgy front tooth . . . (Hey, we were young and in love and you know how it is — anything, even a dodgy tooth, seemed like a sign that we were cosmic twins.)

Eventually we got together and after three months, he asked me to marry him and there was no doubt in my mind when I said yes — I'd known for ages that we were 'meant to be'. I was thirty-one and thought I was terribly mature and wise and told everyone and anyone, 'When you know, you know.'

The night before we got married the priest visited and gave a serious talk about what love really means — he told us about a couple where the man became paralysed from the neck down and his wife had to tend to his every need, and the priest asked us to consider if we'd be willing to do the same. And me, giddy with love and the relief that finally someone was going to marry me, thought, Yes, fine, gotcha! But, of course, I hadn't a clue.

And we were very happy. Everyone had told us that marriage was hard work, but it wasn't. At least not then. I remember, some time in the early days, lying in Himself's arms and thinking, 'I'll never be unhappy again.'

Sometimes I'd read the SoulMates thing in the paper, those brave people putting themselves out there, looking for love, and I'd think, Thank *Christ* I'll never have to do that. Yes, I admit it, I felt rescued and I thought our love was like an entity in itself, if that makes any sense, and it would take care of itself.

There's a lot of talk about Learning To Love Yourself and I always thought it meant going to the cinema on my own or standing in front of the mirror and saying, 'You are a perfect human being, despite being a bit of a fatso.'

But a few years ago, I crash-landed into a Dark Night Of The Soul and my beloved husband couldn't help me and that was *terrifying*. I was entirely alone. It was exactly like when I was in my appalling twenties and waking at four in the morning, feeling abandoned and petrified.

I've talked to other women who've been through similar experiences and the common thread was that we felt, if our husbands couldn't make us feel better, it must mean we didn't love them any more.

But I knew that if I left Himself, I was never getting into another relationship – not only could I never love another man, but how could I, with my appalling thighs, sext anyone?

My Dark Night went on for a couple of horrific years and I begged Himself to leave me and find somebody normal to make him happy.

But he didn't leave – and he'd have been well within his rights to, because the woman he'd fallen in love with had completely disappeared. And I didn't leave, and eventually I re-emerged from the darkness, armed with some valuable insight: Learning To Love Myself means accepting that, as a human being, I will always feel incomplete. That's it. As simple as that. Sometimes my incompleteness will feel like an abyss and at other times I'll barely notice it. But the real nub of 'Loving Myself' means accepting that nothing or nobody outside of myself can fix me. Himself is unbelievably good to me, but fixing me is not his job.

So if I love myself, if I accept *genuinely* that I'm always going to have unpleasant, gnawing emptiness, then *of course* I can love someone else – because they don't have to be perfect, they don't have to rush in and fill up all my emptiness.

Sometimes I see cheesy videos of American weddings where the groom toasts his new bride by declaring, 'You complete me.' And I want to shout, No, no, no, no, no! No one can complete anyone else!

I've a male friend who's forever getting married and is once again contemplating leaving his current wife. He starts every relationship in a flurry of, 'This one is different, this one is perfect!' But when the misfortunate woman transpires to be merely human, he can't forgive her. He decides that because he still feels less than happy, the woman is to blame and he must jettison her and resume his search. And I've a female friend who ended a relationship with a great man because she thought his socks were 'gaudy'. I'm serious.

Because we work together, Himself and I are very close. Also, we couldn't have children, so it's just the two of us. But while he's my best friend by a million miles, he's not my only one because it's not fair and even dangerous to expect one person to meet all of my emotional needs.

So I've my beloved ex-flatmate Suzanne, who I share so much history with, and who isn't into 'Deep and Meaningfuls', but whenever I see her we reminisce over our misspent youths and laugh until we cry. Then I've another friend who does nothing *but* 'Deep and Meaningfuls' and we have great intense discussions about life and love and she makes me feel like a serious person of substance. (I've a bit of a crush on her, to be honest.) And I'm very close to my family and sisters – my mammy lives nearby so I often drop in for half an hour and lie on her couch and eat Mini Magnums and talk rubbish.

Himself also has relationships which don't include me – he goes off with other men to climb mountains and abseil down cliff-faces and eat Snickers. He goes to the football with his brother and his nephew and he's forever off to concerts, because he loves all kinds of music, whereas the only singer I like is George Michael. (Hashtag, Just Being Honest.)

These days Himself and I are closer than we've ever been, but we're older and wiser and a lot less naive about our expectations of each other. However, I loved him a lot when we got married and I love him more now. (But even writing these words puts the fear of God into me that I will be smited with The Curse Of The Smug Woman and that next week Himself will be filmed down a dark alley getting a handjob from a rent-boy.)

All this hard-earned knowledge has helped me reach an equilibrium, a spirit-level between my expectations and reality. Whilst it's disconcerting to discover and experience what it really *means* to be 'only human', one must try and accept it. Acceptance, that's the key to everything, I think. If I can accept that I'll always be imperfect, it makes it easier to accept the imperfection in others, and to love them and myself fully.

32. Nicholas Allan

Nicholas Allan is the author/illustrator of over thirty children's books. His highly original picture books have won him several awards including the Sheffield Children's Book Award for *The Queen's Knickers* and the Federation of Children's Books Best Picture Book Award for *Demon Teddy*. He is also the author of *Hilltop Hospital*, a book that has been adapted into a BAFTA-winning television series.

The Rules of Happiness

When I was little happiness was simple. Happiness was:

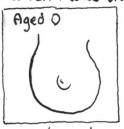

a breast

a red crayon

a wall and a red crayon

a whoopee cushion

The lives, conflicts and inner passions of ants in my ant colony, and stories about them.

It must have been at school I first learnt of The Official Rules of Happiness. I was good at Rules. I was happy.

At art school the Rules were surprisingly similar – even with the drugs.

At the advertising agency I joined the rules were the same. I met Hadley. She was part of the Rules.

How is it possible then that I could have found myself in the Clinic? But that's where I ended up after the divorce. There were no Rules of Happiness at the Clinic.

There was no happiness. I didn't have to work. But I was given paper and paints. I began to use them.

One afternoon I wrote a story about a giant whoopy cushion that invades a Planet of the Ants and changes their lives forever. It eventually found a children's book publisher.

I became a children's author and illustrator. The ruder the stories the happier I am. It's my own Rule of Happiness.

Now I invent new rules all the time. New ones come, old ones go.

The best Rules of Happiness I haven't thought of and are yet to come.

33. Nick Harkaway

Nick Harkaway is the author of *The Gone-Away World*, *Angel-maker* and *Tigerman*. When he's not writing, he spends his time being the husband of a brilliant lawyer and the dad of two small children who are secretly bent on world domination. He likes Italian red wine and lives in a bit of London where the taxis still have a horse at the pointy end.

From Me to You,

I have a bunch of habits of mind that embarrass me, but they get me through the tough days – the days everyone has when you just can't catch a break.

When I was a kid, I was embarrassed that I couldn't do mathematical problems in my head the way some of the other kids could. They heard the problem and they knew how to approach it, they knew what the answers to basic arithmetical problems were. Me, I had to work out that twelve times eight was the same as ten times eight plus two times eight, which meant it was ninety-six. (Since this letter's going in a book, I just checked that on a calculator.) I'm not embarrassed any more. It's not uncool and amateurish to break the numbers down. It's just what works. Some of the fast kids were doing it too, they just did it really quickly.

So I have a bunch of things I do with my head which make my life better. Here's two. You like 'em, they're yours.

1. I draw on my hand.

Yes, I do. In felt tip. I draw a little triangle in whatever colour I feel like to remind me that there are three important things on any ordinary day in my life: my wife, my kids, my new book. There are other people, other tasks, other things to get excited about at other times, but on an average day those are the things that matter. When I draw that triangle, I'm reminding myself that those things get my primetime. Everything else gets what's left of me. I draw it on rather than get it tattooed because I want the deliberate action, the choice, every day. (I worry occasionally that I may gradually be poisoning myself. I'm going to have to buy some pens that write in carrot juice or something.)

The end result is a better version of me, of my responses when I'm exhausted and my son is trying to put a live slug in my ear or my daughter has set fire to the sofa. Drawing the triangle also means I find time to cook something for when my wife gets home and energy to ask about her work rather than just splurging about mine: caring stuff. Simple, and exactly what drops off the agenda when you're tired and stressed, and then suddenly you've forgotten how to do it and your life is that much darker. The point is that you choose your path when it's obvious who you want to be and how you want to behave, at a moment when it's easy. Then when the arse falls out of the trousers and everything is difficult, you've already decided on the high road. It helps. It makes me happier.

(I think it works like those annoying road signs that tell you how fast you're going. Annoying, but check the accident statistics. They do the job, which is why you're seeing more of them.)

Next:

2. I breathe out.

This one is more like being a stereotype from a Hollywood cop movie in which the star's stoned cousin turns up and starts a yoga class in their living room. I don't talk about it because I assume people will think I'm a hippy. Newsflash: I was born in the 70s. In Cornwall. I hung out with a guy who taught me to make pottery, and I pretty much believed *The Hobbit* was a true story until I was fifteen. I'm a hippy.

So I breathe out. I get incredibly frustrated sometimes when I'm not allowed to work. My work is a compulsion. It's also an obligation, and a profession. It's what I do to make money. Because I work from home, a wide and startling variety of people take it upon themselves to task me. I'm home, after all, it's not like being in an office. I also task myself. I go and do the things that need doing, like getting samples of kitchen doors for when we move house. That means sometimes I don't get enough work done and that makes me inwardly furious. It's not just annoying, it undermines my sense of identity. I get cranky to the point where I want to kick a door. (Don't do that. Doors are made of wood and your foot is not.)

So then I breathe out. I tend to see all that pent-up frustration as a black slime in the gap between my ribs, above the stomach. I breathe in air and light, and I let all the badness go out on the exhale, out of my lungs and into the day. Sometimes it spells things in elvish or goblin or whatever. I can't read either of those alphabets, but in my mind's eye I can see letters that clearly mean bad things. Then they blow away and I'm not carrying them any more. Everything is better. My steps are lighter. My mood is sunnier. Try it.

I will say it again: I. Am. A hippy.

Let me add one more observation: I don't think happiness is a single thing and I don't think it's a state you obtain. I think it is the feeling you get from performing your life in a particular mood. It's an action or many actions, and you have to live it and do it all the time and that's how you get to be happy.

These are two of the things I do that help with that. If you do not like them, that is fine. We shall never speak of this day again.

If you do: good.

Triangles. And elvish. They're gonna take away my Mysterious Serious Author card and make me sit with the kids.

Oh, yeah, OK, one more thing: sit with the kids. The grownups are dull.

34. Edward Stourton

Edward Stourton is the author of six books including *Diary of a Dog-Walker* and *Cruel Crossing: Escaping Hitler Across the Pyrenees*. He is writer and presenter of several high-profile current affairs programmes and documentaries for radio and television, and regularly presents BBC Radio 4 programmes such as *The World at One*, *The World This Weekend* and *Analysis*. He is a frequent contributor to the *Today* programme, where for ten years he was one of the main presenters.

If you have lived in a big city – especially London – you will understand how unexpected it was. On our first visit we simply missed it altogether – it was winter, and we were anyway too preoccupied allocating rooms, mentally placing furniture and wondering whether we would manage a mountain of a mortgage.

But when it erupted into leaf at the coming of our first spring, we realised we hadn't really bought a house at all – we had bought a tree with a home attached. It is a copper beech, vast and venerable. The house was built in the 1840s, and I like to think that the tree is the same vintage.

In the high summer its leaves turn a shade that seems outside the spectrum; they absorb the sun and radiate light at the same time. In the chilly opening of 'Little Gidding', one of my favourite poems, T. S. Eliot asks: 'Where is the summer, the unimaginable/zero summer?' The question has always puzzled me, but I now think our copper beech is the answer. It's a contradiction, both dark and full of energy, like a Black Hole.

About five years after we moved in, one of the apple trees caught honey fungus and had to be felled, and we were warned that the copper beech might be infected too; it was like being told you could lose an older friend – an admired teacher, say, or an inspiring boss. Like a pagan, I had come to think of the tree as the guardian of the family's health and happiness.

The shrine for my tree-worshipping is a writing shed we

installed just across the lawn, at the edge of the leaf canopy, when I began to spend more time on books. I wanted a gothic fantasy, so the clever carpenter bought a bus stop, stuck some glass doors on the front and added a few plywood arches to the windows. Because my mind is clearest in the early morning, I try to do an hour's work in the shed before breakfast, and the tree is often the first person I greet each day.

I suspect my love of early starts is a legacy of years working in news; reporters wake up never quite knowing where they will go to bed.

Sometimes the surprises are unwelcome; there've been plenty of missed parties and children's plays, and awkward moments like finding myself on a South Wales miners' picket line still wearing the pinstripe I put on for a Whitehall lunch. But mostly I've relished the excitement that goes with uncertainty; I revelled in all those dawn moments waiting on the doorstep for an airport taxi, and wondering about wherever I was going. Although I travel less now, when I settle in the shed at 6.00 a.m., with a cup of coffee to hand and only the whispering tree for company, I still savour the sense that each day brings limitless possibilities.

But a year before writing this letter I was diagnosed with prostate cancer, and it took a month or so of tests to establish what stage it had reached. For a while the first thought that flashed across my mind each morning wasn't 'what will the day bring' – it was 'I've got cancer' instead.

That changed as soon as the doctors worked out a treatment plan with a cheering prognosis, but it brought home what a blessing it is to have a Tigger-ish disposition at dawn. If I was asked to define unhappiness I think I would say that it is a sense of possibilities closing down instead of opening up – so perhaps happiness is the opposite.

We've never met, and none of this may strike a chord

with you at all. You may – like my wife – be an owl and not a lark. You may have very sound reasons to greet each day with fear and not hope. And you may live a long way away.

But if you are passing, do come and look at the copper beech.

After the honey fungus scare, the tree surgeon – who has thinned it and shaped it over the years, and loves it almost as much as we do – dug a trench in the lawn to check for the sinister black subterranean laces which spread the disease. The soil was clear, so the tree is still bursting into glorious leaf each spring, filling the house with coppery light.

35. Eoin Colfer

Eoin Colfer is the megaselling author of the Artemis Fowl series, *Half Moon Investigations*, *The Supernaturalist*, *Airman* and *The Legend of* . . . books. His brilliant new series, WARP, is out now. Eoin lives with his family in Ireland. www.eoincolfer.com

I believe this letter is intended for someone who is not feeling too happy, and that the person reading the letter might actually be the person the advice is meant for.

If that person is you, you might be asking yourself: what does this guy know about giving advice to people who are depressed? What does he have to get depressed about? He's a hugely successful author and incredibly handsome to boot. Not to mention that he probably could still play professional football with a couple of days' training, and has a beard that is as verdant as that of Zeus himself. He spends his days writing leprechaun stories and counting his money. So what in the name of the holy trinity (Barry, Maurice, Robin) does he know about depression?

Well, I know.

That's the thing about depression. It doesn't care who you are or what you've got. Depression is like a dark cloud that can settle on any hilltop. No, wait, I've got a better simile: depression is like a Brighton seagull. It doesn't care who it poops on.

I think depression has a dodgy reputation because it usually comes to our attention via the gossip mags, i.e. Permatanned WAG Breaks Her Silence Over Battle With Depression. No disrespect to perma-tanned WAGs, as I said, depression is like a Brighton seagull and so on. Another problem is that depression is invisible, and so often people can secretly suspect that the sufferer is just looking for atten-tion, especially if their life looks pretty good from the outside.

But we all put our brave face on in public. What's going on behind the smiley face is often a different story.

I don't know you and you don't know me, but who really knows anybody?

Sometimes I look into the faces of my nearest and dearest and think to myself: I have no idea what's going on behind those eyes. And I don't because everyone has a private side that they keep hidden away from other people. I certainly do. I have thoughts and ideas every day that I would never dream of communicating to other people in case I would be summarily judged and executed. And no matter how often I am told that I shouldn't worry about what other people think about me, I think a person would have to be made of stone not to be affected by other people's opinions. So thanks a bunch, Internet.

Now comes the advice part. Again, you are probably sceptical about taking advice from the leprechaun guy, and I am certainly not claiming to have some Gandalfian wisdom to bestow upon you. All I can do is tell you what helped me in my quest for happiness.

I could trot out the old chestnut: *you are not alone.*

But I won't, because you could be alone. Sitting in a room somewhere with all sorts of thoughts chasing themselves around your head.

So if you are in that room, locked into destructive trains of thought, I am sure there are hundreds of coping strategies that you could turn to, I have turned to most of them myself, but the one that worked for me was writing.

I know, I write kids' fantasy stuff mostly, so how in the name of Larry Ernest Blackmon's codpiece (look it up) could that help with depression? Well firstly writing it took my mind off myself and, believe me, I was fed up hating myself for being depressed with no good reason. Secondly, I discovered that in spite of the light-hearted subject matter, I was able to sneak some of my personal dark thoughts in between the lines, which helped exorcise them a little bit. And thirdly, writing is an activity. And activity is the nemesis of depression and the friend of happiness. So I write as much as I can, because

I'd rather have happiness, neck pain, back pain and repetitive stress disorder than depression any day of the week.

So, my advice in a nutshell is to have a crack at writing in some form. No need for a trilogy about a very sad unicorn who is a thinly veiled version of yourself. You can if you want to, but I find poetry is good. Too arty-farty? Try a blog or a diary. Write a letter to a friend. Write a letter to yourself. Get on social media and update your status from *bored* to *fabulous*. Join a writers' group. Work on your novel. Write a one-act play. This is an excellent way to bring issues into the open and, trust me, theatre-goers love *issues*. So if you don't have any, invent some.

Physical exercise is probably also good but I missed that particular treadmill. Someone else will have to write the *joys of the mini-marathon* letter. Put a pen to paper for god's sake. Put a finger to key. You don't have to be any good and you probably won't be on the first hundred tries. But that doesn't matter, it's not about being good. It's about being occupied. It's about getting those neurons excited over something external rather than internal.

I am not saying writing is a magic happy pill, or that it will work for everybody. But it worked for me and continues to work, and is especially good if you do happen to be alone.

And if you're looking for a place to start with your first short story, let me help you out with a first line. I usually charge a fortune for these because they're so genius, but you can have this one for free:

Once upon a time, in a faraway land called Melancholios, there lived a brave non-gender specified knight who decided that it was high time to find out, for once and for all, if the pen really was mightier than the sword . . .

Finish in your own words.

36. Shirley Hughes

Shirley Hughes is the illustrator of the much-loved Dogger and the Alfie series. She first began to write and draw her picture books when her children were young. Her first book, *Lucy and Tom's Day*, was published in 1960. Shirley Hughes has won several awards, including the Eleanor Farjeon Award, and the Kate Greenaway Medal for Illustration. Shirley received an OBE in 1999 for services to Children's Literature.

There is nothing so exciting, or so intimidating, as a blank piece of paper. When I am working, if things are going well, and I have got hold of a brush which is just right and the washes are flowing sweetly, everything from world concerns to family cares goes quite out of my mind. My sketchbooks lie open around the workroom. I keep returning to them, and other inspiring references, for inspiration. They, like my first rough dummy, are a lynchpin. I hang on to them all the way. Tapping into this freedom, the excitement generated by these first drawings and translating it successfully, is the driving force. However well you manage to realise your inner vision, at the end of the day you just have to hope that you can take Ernest Hemingway's advice and leave it when you're going good. And, even though I know I haven't a hope of creating the images that were there in my head, attempting to is still the nearest thing I know to flying into the sun.

Alfie

with love from Shirley Hughes

Original illustration by Shirley Hughes for *Dear Stranger*

37. Sathnam Sanghera

Sathnam Sanghera was born in 1976. He is an award-winning writer for *The Times*. His first book, *The Boy with the Topknot*, was shortlisted for the 2008 Costa Biography Award and the 2009 PEN/Ackerley Prize and named 2009 Mind Book of the Year. His novel *Marriage Material* was shortlisted for the 2014 South Bank Sky Arts Award for Literature and the 2013 Costa First Novel Award.

Dear Wolverhampton Asian Goth,

You don't know me, and I don't know you, but I saw you sitting there, in Costa, dressed in black, early Leonard Cohen leaking from your headphones, croissant crumbs littering your paperback, a nearby group of lads tossing Wotsits at your head, and felt the need to write.

I'd like to say you reminded me of me as a teenager. But while it is the destiny of all melancholic, literary youths in the provinces to vaguely resemble Adrian Mole, the fact is that I could only have dreamed of being as cool as you. As a child of Indian immigrants, I didn't have educated or socially integrated relatives, let alone the Internet, to guide my taste in those days, and was therefore completely at the mercy of Radio 1 and reduced to getting my melancholic hits from the likes of Phil Collins and Richard Marx. There were no coffee shops in Wolverhampton in the 80s and 90s – all our hanging out being done on street corners, in alleyways, libraries and in Wolverhampton bus station. Also, Asian goths weren't a thing then – dressing in lace and black and purple with the intention of vaguely resembling a seventeeth-century syphilitic poet being an activity that, like football, journalism, acting and unsliced bread, was pursued almost exclusively by white people.

And in saying that I realise I may sound like I'm slipping into one of the traps and clichés of ageing: the overwhelming desire to tell people younger than yourself how fortunate they are. But that is not my intention. I envy you for a whole load of things – for your mascara-application skills, for having a family that let you leave home looking like that (at the very least, my mother would have washed those jeans or made me iron that T-shirt), and for not having to grow up in a town where working men's clubs have colour bars and the local football fans are known for going about sporting KKK hoods. But your third generation world is more complex than mine ever was, and ambiguity is hard to navigate.

I simply wanted to write to say that as grim as life may seem now, with those losers backcombing their hair to mimic you, and reading out the cover quotes from your copy of Jorge Luis Borges' *Labyrinths* as if they were John Gielgud on stage at the Birmingham Rep, and taking the piss out of your black streaks of eyeliner and army surplus combat boots, everything is going to be OK. Not least because you have already learned an important survival skill, which, judging by their identikit Ted Baker clothing, lame banter and weak efforts to follow the fad for facial hair, despite their inability to actually grow beards or moustaches of any variety, those lads have not. Namely, the art of being different.

So much human misery is caused by people trying to fit into holes they don't belong. Whether it is hiding their sexuality, or hanging out socially with people they don't even like, or going along with stuff just because of social and family pressure to do so. But you're already there. It is almost certain that you will not remain as you are, but you already have the courage to be different. You're decades, and in some cases, a lifetime, ahead of most people.

The other quality that I know is going to hold you in good stead is that you have a brain. Of course, I don't actually know you and it's possible I'm projecting intelligence upon you. But in my experience, the dim do not often have Nietzsche quotes tattooed onto their hands, or listen to Nick Drake, or sit around annotating copies of seminal magic realist prose. It's not an easy path to choose a life of the mind – I was the first person in my family to own a book, and cousins literally came from miles around to admire it, laugh at it, and enquire sarcastically if I was planning to follow it up with the purchase of a top hat and a home study course in Latin. But sticking to books was the best thing I ever did. For it was books that made me appreciate that while everything matters, nothing matters that much, that the best things in life (nature, people, art) are free, that most of the things people worry about don't end up happening, and that with writing, you'll never really be alone.

The other realisation that books will, I hope, lead you towards is that life, for most people, gets better, as they get older. I'm not sure, to be honest, about the nature of your melancholic state, whether it chose you, or you chose it, or even if you're, technically speaking, a goth and an emo. I've just googled the difference between the two and the Urban Dictionary tells me that 'goth is when you hate the world' and 'emo is when the world hates you'. I hope neither is true for you, that you are just indulging in the comfort of self-imposed adolescent misery, which, after all, is the only sane response to your situation, being stuck in a town where people pronounce 'cup of tea' as 'kipper tie' and lattes as 'lar-tays', where members of the public, in 2015, try to order kebabs in coffee shops, and where complete strangers mock you for daring to read a book in public.

But those lads are being thrown out now for consuming 'non-brand' goods, and I'm pretty sure the girl who is chucking them out fancies you (you should ask her out), and even Wolverhampton has changed miles for the better in the decades since I left, and soon you will be free too. See where despondency takes you, but be careful not to let it claim you, or blind you to the excitement and adventure that awaits.

Yours,
Sathnam

38. Alexandra Fuller

Alexandra Fuller is the author of the international bestseller *Don't Let's Go To The Dogs Tonight* and *Leaving Before the Rains Come*. She was born in England in 1969 and, in 1972, moved with her family to a farm in southern Africa. She lived in Africa until her mid-twenties. In 1994, she moved to Wyoming. She has three children.

Letter one

Dear Stranger,

I agreed to write to you about happiness because I
thought it would be a nice, worthy, simple task
(forgive me, if you can, for that arrogance). But
seriously, what could go wrong? For starters, I am not
supposed to know you, so what can it matter what
you think of me, or of what I say? And if you are a
stranger to me, then I am a stranger to you. And so
who are we to begin to speak to one another, or to
hear one another?

Oh, who are we? Are we?

Are we the two strangers in the Denver/London/
Nairobi airport, angry and tired and flight-delayed?
Are we the two strangers at the fireworks display;
you are cheering, I am cringing (or the other way
around)? Are you the person hopping up and down in
your car in New York/London/Lusaka because I have
accidentally, or purposefully, taken your parking
spot? Are you the mother of the little boy who will
one day grow into the man who will do something so
unthinkably sad, or so unthinkably glorious, that your
name will be for ever (un)holy?

This question kept me up at night.

Then I remembered what I have always known, but
what I have been taught to forget.

You're everyone, technically. You're you, and my
children, and the man with whom I share my bed,
and the woman who will take this letter from me in

the morning and put it on the lorry to Rock Springs. And you're the oil-rig worker in Rock Springs who drills for the oil that goes into the lorry that will take this letter to the plane that will be flown by the pilot who is the angry, tired person at the Denver/London/Nairobi airport.

You see where this can never end? Like William Butler Yeats said, there are no strangers, just friends one has yet to meet. Or even enemies one has yet to meet. But nonetheless, there you are, a piece of me. And here am I, a piece of you.

So, before I even get to the happiness bit of this exercise, at least half the premise of this letter has already dissolved.

There is no 'Dear Stranger'.

There is only, 'Dear You, Me, Us'.

Love,
Alexandra

Therefore.

Letter two

Dear You/Me/Us,

This is laughable. A philosopher who is also a monk wrote a whole book about Happiness and I read it in pursuit of that thing, and I am past the point at which there is any hope of pretending I have more than half my life left in which to figure this out, and I have met only one or two happy people in my whole life (of whom that philosopher/monk was one). Which is not a good thing, or a bad thing. But it is a thing. So who am I to write about happiness when I have had only flashes of it myself, and yet I would not say I was an unhappy person, at all.

I just am.

Like a duck on an ocean. I bob about. Sometimes I
believe myself to be happy. Other times, I look out at
all the whole nothingness of everything, and I can't
get over myself fast enough for the next wave to be
nothing but a wave instead of an internal tide.

Happiness is a difficult thing to have; maybe it's
even impossible. You, or I, can't possess it any more
than we can hold on to time, or air, or water or any
of the other things that are essential to life. In my
experience, happiness is that fraction of a moment
when what I think, and how I feel, and what I do all
line up, and I feel bigger than the small spiral of my
thinking. I feel, in other words, alive, which is
perhaps just another way of saying aware –
equanimously aware – so that things are not bad, or
good, but simply there, wanted or unwanted perhaps,
but there nonetheless. And I am no longer allowed to
ignore the pain and pleasure of being alive.

Wave comes. Waves go. Nothing is for ever. Nothing.
Everything changes. Everything. Sometimes, I say
that to myself over and over. Just like that. And a few
times in my life, I have sat for ten days straight and
said something like it over and over until everything
dissolves into the moment. In those times, my whole
soul could fly away for half an hour on the sheer
bright unexpected gorgeous beauty of worm washed
pinkly wet to the earth's surface on the path between
the meditation hall and the dormitories at the austere
retreat centre where I had sequestered myself.

On the other hand, the way I see it, happiness's
absence is a sort of un-aliveness, as if the world has
been leached grey, and my soul has washed out in
that greyness. And now there is a sharp and
screaming sense that some things are absolutely bad
and some things are unequivocally good, and I cringe
from the tender, the raw, the difficult and become
addicted to numbness. I become unable to name my

feelings and they grow until they are mostly all I am. I am one very reactive, fragile person. I feel sorry for myself. And that, in my experience, is the beginning of my way out of happiness's absence.

Just feel. Again. A lot.

So.

My favourite question is not 'Are you happy?' but rather something I read by the Haitian writer Edwidge Danticat (who knows a thing or two about happiness and its absence): 'There is always a place where, if you listen closely in the night, you will hear a mother telling a story and at the end of the tale, she will ask you this question: "Ou libéré?" Are you free, my daughter?'

That is all.

My dear sweet Me, You, Us.

Are you free, my friend?

Love,
Alexandra

39. Daniel J. Levitin

Dr. Daniel J. Levitin has a PhD in Psychology, training at Stanford University Medical School and UC Berkeley. Currently he is Dean of Arts & Humanities at the Minerva Schools at KGI in San Francisco, California, and a Professor of Psychology, Behavioural Neuroscience and Music at McGill University in Montreal, Canada. He is the author of three no. 1 bestselling books: *This is Your Brain On Music*, *The World in Six Songs* and *The Organized Mind*.

Dear Stranger,

You don't know me. I'm a scientist and an artist – I know, a very strange combination – but through these intersecting interests I've learned something about happiness and how to claim it. It is not always easy to become happy at the snap of a finger. Fortunately science and art have something to say about this.

When we're depressed or unhappy, we typically feel cut off from other people. We feel alone, misunderstood. The last thing we want is for someone to come storming into the room with an irritatingly chirpy manner, telling us to get up off the couch and stop feeling sorry for ourselves. We don't want to watch a parade, and we *really* don't want to listen to happy music. These serve to make us feel even more strongly that other people don't understand what we're feeling. But listening to sad music in this state often makes us feel better. Perhaps not right away, but sooner than you'd think. This seems paradoxical! Happy music makes us more depressed and sad music makes us happy? What kind of weird neurochemical mechanism does that?

Sadness is an evolutionary response to something that has gone wrong in our lives (or at least our perception that something has gone wrong). Taking some down time, some quiet time alone to reflect on our situation allows us the chance to figure out what went wrong, to nurse our wounds (both physical and emotional) and come back smarter than before. Prolactin, a tranquilising and soothing hormone, is one of the neurochemical responses to sadness. Prolactin is also released after orgasm, after birth, and in mothers while they nurse their infants. A chemical analysis of tears reveals that prolactin is not always present in tears – it is not released in tears that lubricate the eye, or when the eye is irritated, or in tears of joy; it is only released in tears of sorrow. Sad music allows us to 'trick' our brain into releasing prolactin in response to the safe or imaginary sorrow induced by the music, and the prolactin then turns around our mood.

There's a psychological angle as well. When we listen to a sad song we identify with the composer and musicians. When we put on the right piece of sad music we realise *that's how I feel too!* We're no longer alone sitting at the edge of the cliff – we realise that there is someone there with us who has experienced the same things. And not only that but she has come back from that state and turned the experience into a beautiful work of art.

Not everyone agrees about which pieces of music are sad. Musical tastes are very individual and idiosyncratic, and a piece that strikes us as sad one day may seem happy on another day. The key is to follow your intuition. Also, plan ahead. Make a list of songs that you find sad and comforting at the same time so that you can turn to them when you need them, especially because you might find you're not in the mood to rummage around for anything.

Music has been a part of human life for millennia. Some of the oldest artefacts discovered in human (and even

Neanderthal) burial sites are musical instruments. There is no known culture now or anytime in the past that lacked music. Music is part of our cultural and biological heritage. It can delight, infuriate, depress, yet it can also soothe and comfort. Feeling sad? Take two Joni Mitchells and call me in the morning.

40. Claire Greaves

Claire Greaves speaks publicly about her battle with mental illness through radio, television and social media. She also writes a blog: mentalillnesstalk.wordpress.com.

I don't know you but I have an important message for you. A message of hope. I never thought that I would be in a position where I felt hopeful, let alone share my hope with others. I was always the one on the other end of the message shrugging off the 'hope givers' and telling them that they didn't understand because I was different from other people, it would never get better for me. I didn't think that I would ever feel happiness again, I used to doubt that true happiness even existed and if you would've told me twelve months ago that I would smile a genuine smile I wouldn't have believed you, in fact I would've argued with you. I was fixated on ending my life, utterly convinced that it was the only way that life could get better for me and for everyone around me. I felt that I ruined my family's lives and that I was a burden upon every person I encountered. I came scarily close to dying and for a long time I despised the fact that I was saved. Today I am glad that I survived, life is amazing. Not only has my life improved but I have used my life to improve the lives of others. My life feels meaningful. The buzz I get from life makes all the suffering of the last decade worth it, the physical and mental agony, the hospital admissions and the people who didn't understand. In the end my living nightmare led to me achieving my dreams. The best days of my life have happened as a direct result of my worst days and that gives me hope that when things are awful and unbearable it is for a reason, and maybe that reason isn't clear at the time but eventually it will be.

People told me that I wouldn't feel better overnight, but

I did. One day I was my usual unwell and deeply hopeless self, truly believing life wasn't for me and convinced each year was my last because my illness would push me to death. The weight of depression was crushing my bones. It was dark and anorexia made it so very cold. I felt like I was screaming but the sound wasn't leaving my lips. I thought I was trapped with no way out but then an opportunity came along that I never expected to happen to me and I felt free and alive for the first time. I put music on, danced, then I looked at myself in the mirror and said, 'Oh my gosh, life is amazing!' over and over again. I held on to that feeling through all the opportunities to come and it felt like I was riding life on a magic carpet, sometimes it would drop a bit lower but mainly it was at a perfect mid-point between total euphoria and depression. I've reached a point where I am able to both live and enjoy my life. I am still ill, it is still a daily battle, but I am happy and I haven't been able to say that for over a decade.

The society that we live in sends out incorrect messages about happiness. Adverts convince us that we will be happy if we have the most fashionable clothes, the biggest TV and the body of a supermodel. We are constantly bombarded with images of smiling faces owning materialistic items but materialism isn't happiness. I could have the car, drink and mobile phone that I see on TV and I could still feel despair. Happiness is about creating memories and loving others. Happiness is your dog greeting you with a wagging tail when you return home or a mother's kiss goodnight. Money cannot buy meaningful feelings, money can only buy a short-term fix.

We live in a society hungry for drama and this is reflected in the news, we are only ever told about the negatives: deaths, terror threats, violence and car crashes. What about the life savers, the fundraisers, the scientist who had a breakthrough? There's plenty of good in the world but strangely it isn't spoken about. If you're feeling happy never hide it. Post that selfie, tweet about it. Happiness can be contagious, it takes one person to start spreading it and can be passed on through something as simple as a smile. Little acts of kindness and love, compliments, a hand to hold, all those little things that restore hope in humanity and remind us life is good. Allow happiness to beam out of you and see how many people catch it.

I know sometimes it can feel like happiness is a long way away, maybe you can't even see it, maybe you've forgotten what it feels like but it is there and you will find it one day, probably when you least expect it. Happiness isn't about being well or life being perfect, it's those moments that restore your spirit and personality and push you to fight through difficult times. Those moments that make you want to scream 'I am alive'.

I never thought I'd have friends but now I am able to talk and laugh and plan trips to London with them. I am able to sit on the sofa with my beautiful family and howl with laughter at comedians on TV. Nothing feels better than laughing until tears run down your face and your cheek muscles ache. I never thought that I would receive messages from people thanking me for helping them and that there would be a list on my desk with places I want to go and things I want to do rather than suicide plans hidden in the drawers.

After a very long time of mental illness my life improved in a very short amount of time. It doesn't matter who you are or what you are going through, there is always hope.

For as long as there is life, there is hope.

41. Arianna Huffington

Arianna Huffington is the chair, president, and editor-in-chief of the Huffington Post Media Group, and author of fourteen books. In May 2005, she launched the *Huffington Post*, a news and blog site that quickly became one of the most widely-read, linked-to, and frequently-cited media brands on the internet. In 2012, the site won a Pulitzer Prize for national reporting. She has been named on *Time Magazine's* list of The 100 Most Influential People in the World and the *Forbes* Most Powerful Women list. Originally from Greece, she moved to England when she was sixteen and graduated from Cambridge University with an MA in economics. At twenty-one, she became president of the famed debating society, the Cambridge Union. Her fourteenth book, *Thrive: The Third Metric to Redefining Success and Creating a Life of Well-Being, Wisdom, and Wonder* debuted at no. 1 on the *New York Times* Bestseller list and was released in paperback in March 2015.

Even though we don't know each other, I'm somehow certain that we share a longing to understand what it means to lead a 'good life' and experience happiness in a way that goes beyond just accumulating victories or trophies, and to feel like we're part of something larger than ourselves.

I'm convinced of two fundamental truths about human beings. The first is that we all have within us a centred place of wisdom, harmony and strength. This is a truth that all the world's philosophies and religions – whether Christianity, Islam, Judaism or Buddhism – acknowledge in one form or another: 'The kingdom of God is within you.' Or as Archimedes said, 'Give me a place to stand, and I will move the world.'

The second truth is that we're all going to veer away from that place again and again and again. That's the nature of life. In fact, we may be off course more often than we are on course. The question is how quickly can we get back to that centred place of wisdom, harmony and strength. It's in this sacred place that life is transformed from struggle to grace, and we are suddenly filled with trust, whatever our obstacles, challenges or disappointments. As Steve Jobs said in his now legendary commencement address at Stanford: 'You can't connect the dots looking forward; you can only connect them looking backwards. So you have to trust that the dots will somehow connect in your future. You have to trust in something – your gut, destiny, life, karma, whatever. This approach has never let me down, and it has made all the difference in my life.'

There is a purpose to our lives, even if it is sometimes hidden from us, and even if the biggest turning points and heartbreaks only make sense as we look back, rather than as we are experiencing them. So we might as well live life as if – as the poet Rumi put it – everything is rigged in our favour.

We all have within us the ability to move from struggle to grace, whatever the challenges we encounter. When we are in that 'bubble of grace', it doesn't mean that the every-day things that used to bother, irritate and upset us disappear; they don't, but they no longer have the power to bother, irritate or upset us. And when the really hard things come our way – death, sickness, loss – we are better able to deal with them instead of being overwhelmed by them.

I faced one such big test on March 4, 2012. That's the day I got the sort of call every parent dreads more than anything else: 'Mommy, I can't breathe.' It was Christina, my oldest daughter, in her senior year at Yale, two months away from graduating.

Looking back on that March day as I was frantically driving from New York to the emergency room in New Haven, and later when we left the emergency room with my sedated daughter crying in my arms, and later still over the hard weeks that followed, I focused on all that I was grateful for: that my daughter was alive, that she had a lov-ing family that rallied around her, and that she wanted to get well. Christina had struggled with drugs before, but we had thought that was behind her. And never before had it gotten to this point.

Everything else I had thought was important in my life fell away. Over the next year, until Christina decided to go public with her addiction, only our family, her closest friends, and my daughters' godmothers knew. I felt like it was her story and her life – and, therefore, her decision if and when to talk about it. I was proud of her when, thirteen months later, she decided to write about her struggle.

Learning to be vulnerable without shame and accepting our emotions without judgement becomes much easier when we realise that we are more than our emotions, our thoughts, our fears and our personalities. And the stronger the realisation, the easier it becomes to move from struggle to grace.

42. Richard Branson

Sir Richard Branson is a hugely successful international entrepreneur, adventurer and icon, and is founder of the Virgin Group. His autobiography, *Losing My Virginity*, and his books on business, *Screw It, Let's Do It, Business Stripped Bare, Screw Business as Usual* and *Like a Virgin* are all international bestsellers. He lives on Necker Island in the British Virgin Islands and is married to Joan and has two grown-up children – Holly and Sam.

Dear Stranger,

You don't know me but . . . I hear you are going
through a tough time, and I would like to help you. I
want to be open and honest with you, and let you
know that happiness isn't something just afforded to
a special few. It can be yours, if you take the time to
let it grow.

It's OK to be stressed, scared and sad – I certainly
have been throughout my sixty-five years. I've
confronted my biggest fears time and time again. I've
cheated death on many adventures, seen loved ones
pass away, failed in business, minced my words in
front of tough audiences, and had my heart broken.

I know I'm fortunate to live an extraordinary life,
and that most people would assume my business
success and the wealth that comes with it have
brought me happiness. But they haven't; in fact it's
the reverse. I am successful, wealthy and connected
because I am happy.

So many people get caught up in doing what they
think will make them happy but, in my opinion, this
is where they fail. Happiness is not about doing, it's
about being. In order to be happy, you need to think
consciously about it. Don't forget the to-do list, but
remember to write a to-be list too.

Kids are often asked: 'What do you want to be
when you grow up?' The world expects grandiose
aspirations: 'I want to be a writer, a doctor, the prime
minister.' They're told: go to school, go to college, get a
job, get married, and then you'll be happy. But that's

all about doing, not being – and while doing will bring
you moments of joy, it won't necessarily reward you
with lasting happiness.

Stop and breathe. Smell the roses. Listen to a child
laugh. Sing in the shower. Turn your head to the sky
on a crisp summer day. Be healthy. Be around your
friends and family. Be there for someone, and let
someone be there for you. Be bold. Just be for a
minute.

If you allow yourself to be in the moment, and
appreciate the moment, happiness will follow.

I speak from experience. We've built a business
empire, joined conversations about the future of our
planet, attended many memorable parties and met
many unforgettable people. And while these things
have brought me great joy, it's the moments that I
stopped just to be, rather than do, that have given me
true happiness. Why? Because allowing yourself just
to be, puts things into perspective. Try it. Be still. Be
present.

It's watching the flamingos fly across Necker Island
at dusk. It's holding my new grandchildren's tiny
hands. It's looking up at the stars and dreaming of
seeing them up close one day. It's listening to my
family's dinner-time debates. It's the smile on a
stranger's face, the smell of rain, the ripple of a wave,
the wind across the sand. It's the first snow fall of
winter, and the last storm of summer.

There's a reason we're called human beings and not
human doings. As human beings we have the ability
to think, move and communicate in a heightened way.
We can cooperate, understand, reconcile and love –
that's what sets us apart from most other species.
Don't waste your human talents by stressing about
nominal things, or that which you cannot change. If
you take the time simply to be and appreciate the
fruits of life, your stresses will begin to dissolve, and
you will be happier.

But don't just seek happiness when you're down. Happiness shouldn't be a goal, it should be a habit. Take the focus off doing, and start being every day. Be loving, be grateful, be helpful, and be a spectator to your own thoughts.

Allow yourself to be in the moment, and appreciate the moment. Take the focus off everything you think you need to do, and start being – I promise you, happiness will follow.

Happy regards,
Richard Branson

43. Molly Pearce
(The Doodle Chronicles)

Molly Pearce is a postgraduate student and creator of The Doodle Chronicles, an initiative that uses simple doodles to document her journey with severe clinical depression and an anxiety disorder. Her doodles have been featured by mental health charities and media outlets, including as part of the *Guardian*'s Christmas Appeal and a recent feature on BBC Radio 5 Live.

You don't know me but I am only too aware of the multitude of things that a smile can hide. Having hidden severe mental illness behind a smile for almost a decade, I learned how to act as if I was happy but never to actually feel it. As my acting improved over the years, my mental health deteriorated with no one any the wiser. It was only once I could no longer hide my struggles, once I reached crisis point and had no option but to seek help, that I realised that I didn't have to suffer in silence. Choosing to stop acting and break the silence was the first step on a journey towards improved mental health.

'Behind a Smile' was one of my first doodles and one that, sadly, seems to have hit home with many. I drew it in the hope that it would help those who have never experienced mental illness to understand that, although often invisible, it is serious and life-changing. I also hope that this doodle and my story can help everyone struggling to know that they are not alone and that they don't have to struggle in silence: even if you aren't ready to talk to friends and family, please seek professional help, contact a charity, phone a helpline or reach out anonymously on social media. There is so much support available, professional and otherwise. You deserve to get the help you need and feel supported. Happiness is out there for us all, some of us just might need a bit of extra help and care to get there.

With love,
Molly

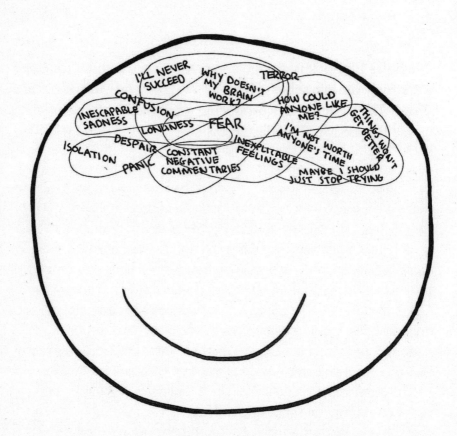

You never know what hides
behind a smile.

44. Nicholas Pinnock

Nicholas Pinnock is a stage and screen actor known for Sky Atlantic's drama series *Fortitude*, *Top Boy* and *Mandela: The Prison Years*. Nicholas is producing a book of poetry and is a judge for the Mind Media Awards.

. . . Hey,

How are you today? I hope well and in good health. Physical and mental. You know, not a day goes by without me thinking about you and how you're doing. You're constantly on my mind and in my well wishes because I know how you may be feeling at times. I know, first hand, what some of your days, weeks or months feel like. I understand what you go through. What it feels like to get out of bed some days. What it feels like to face yourself in the mirror. What it feels like to push break-fast around on a plate. What it feels like to get out of the house. What it feels like to face the throng of people on your way to work. What it feels like to hold it together once at work. What it feels like not being able to eat your lunch at the given lunch-time. What it feels like to deal with things during that day. What it feels like to see people's lips move while all you can hear are the voices in your head. What it feels like to get back in that throng on your way to your safe haven. What it feels like to get home and shut that door behind you. What it feels like to take the day off, layer by layer. What it feels like to get back into bed and all the while wishing you'd never left . . . I know we prob-ably won't always see eye to eye and there are times when we just can't stand the sight of another human being but ultim-ately, I have nothing but the purest of Love that human beings can have for each other. And I give it you. Why am I telling you this? . . . Because it's important to reach out to each other from time to time. To share. To share the fact that you're not on your own . . . And believe me, you're not.

I wrote a poem one day and although I knew why I wrote it, what I didn't know, until now, was who I wrote it for . . . Now I do . . .

You've Seen The Place

. . . I've seen the place where forever calls.
I've felt the sunshine when it's the rain that Falls.

Letting go is a very hard thing to do.
But holding it all in is just not good for you.

There is a love in me that speaks its truth About all I
    believe in.
Belief in that truth has made for my constant Achieving.

Peeping through the window of my Tomorrows:
My curiosity knows no boundaries for such Excitement.
The death of my yesterdays has led to my Knowing just
    what my former lives have Meant.

We all want too much but when we get it, it's Never
    enough.
For we've never run scared and we've never Slept rough.

Our children hold the answers to Everything . . . but
    should everything be Questioned?

Have I failed to mention . . .
Laughter and Love are what keep you alive When the
    world and your life are trying to kill You.

Brothers and Sisters . . . true Love!
O' is ours to embrace.
And you can't deny the infectious reaction of Laughter
    on a child's face.

The eeny, the meeny, the miny, the moe.
I don't know anything that you don't know.

The hands of time will teach us this in years.
But some lessons learned, may result in our Tears.

We're all one and the same . . .
. . . and the same applies to all.
We're universally connected. Listen . . . can You hear
    its call?

. . . The rhythm of the heartbeat is felt in Everyone.
So why hate, discriminate, aggravate and Spoil all the fun?

We need not fight one another to the death.
Instead we should comfort those, as they Take their
    last breath.

Let's stand together and combine our love to
    Become one.
With such conscious, positive energy we can Live on
    and ever strong.

The night-ness of our day-to-day can cloud Even to
    oldest of souls to believing much a False truth.
Which is why we need to connect back, to The
    instinctive-ness of our inner youth.

In the oasis of our minds is where we can Clearly see . . .
. . . the wonders of this life that the Universe Has gifted
  to you and me . . .

You've seen the place where forever calls . . .
You too have felt the sunshine when it's the Rain that
  falls . . .

Stay Blessed. Keep Smiling. Dream Happy . . .

N. x

45. Tim Smit

Sir Tim Smit has lived in Cornwall since 1987 when, together with John Nelson, he 'discovered' and then restored the Lost Gardens of Heligan. He remains a director of the gardens and is Executive Vice-Chairman and co-founder of the award-winning Eden Project. He has received a variety of national awards, including the Royal Society of Arts Albert Medal, an honorary CBE in 2002, and an honorary KBE in 2011. This appointment was made substantive in June 2012 when he became a British Citizen. He was voted 'Great Briton of 2007' in the Environment category of the Morgan Stanley Great Britons Awards.

Hello.

We don't know each other so congratulations, you now share something with truck drivers and barmaids. That secular priesthood, those keepers of the anonymous confessional, offering the comfort of strangers to any who would bare their souls. They know a thing or two about happiness, or at least what others think would make them so. When they download, their truth is a world full of...

If only I had, if only I could, I just wish... if I could turn the clock back, I would do things, great things, wonderful deeds, I would follow my heart and live up to the standards set for my heroes, by me and you know what? I would be happy. I would be happy with champagne in my veins, I would feel satisfied, I would be the person I know I was meant to be.

Fools, all of them. As Gertrude Stein once said, 'the problem with getting there, is that when you get there, there is no there... there'.

I know, I have been to there. It turned to dust in my hands and blew away on the wind of my desperate hope for happiness. Success is a lonely place, no one loves you there, least of all yourself. If I was on my deathbed wishing to relive again that which pleased me deeply, it would be swimming naked by moonlight – in company. It would be the grit of sand between my toes and the taste of salt on my lips; I would dream cocoa with rum on a cold winter's night where the breath hurts your lungs and snow's on the ground; the delicious anticipation of Sunday newspapers and good coffee and time, yes time, in the company of people, not just those you love, but those whose curiosity in life lights you up. I'll draw a veil over the joys of love, for each of us has our moments and to reveal is to betray, but . . . what can beat a gentle breeze through open windows like a gentle caress on glowing naked skin?

I see no Oscars, or glittering prizes here, no time for a bucket list of things to see and do before the great goodbye. I'd like to think I had the imagination to dream of what I cannot see or get to. I'd rather dream of my fishing float dipping beneath the surface of the pond, or the breathless 'walk of death' along the branch of a Wellingtonia, before reaching safety, heart racing and feeling so alive; or the thrill of anticipation before the band hits its first chord and children and, I admit it, grandchildren making me laugh.

Paradise is over-rated. Eve was restless in Eden and wanted out. Odysseus, rather than wanting to stay with Circe on her magic island, preferred to return to the barren rocks of Ithaca. Us humans can't take too much of a good thing, it poisons the soul. Gardeners perhaps understand happiness as that moment, that rare moment of repose when nature yields her bounty and all is well. Happiness here is knowing that this beauty is transient, but that through your labours you made it so and, in that moment, you are happy and so . . . with love. It is not a condition that is of itself happy, like the garden, it needs continuous tending, creating moments . . . so the lesson is ignore the cruel, the negative, the ungenerous, when in doubt favour the kind, the thoughtful and what you hope is true . . . But when all is said, dare to follow your heart, because it usually doesn't lie even if your voice hasn't the courage to speak on its behalf.

So, stranger, I hope life throws the dice in your favour and even if it doesn't, makes it interesting.

Good luck.

46. Tony Parsons

Tony Parsons left school at sixteen and was working on the night shift at Gordon's Gin Distillery when he landed his first job in journalism on the *New Musical Express*. Since then he has become an award-winning journalist and a bestselling novelist. His most recent books are his crime novels *The Murder Bag* and *The Slaughter Man*, featuring DC Max Wolfe.

You don't know me but this I know – we should enjoy every sandwich. That is the key, the secret, the one true path to genuine happiness – to not be bound by the vanished past, or in thrall to a future that might never happen. But to live our fleeting lives in the here and now. It is our best shot at real happiness.

We spend so much time on what we can't control, in our wounds from the past and our hopes for the future. And that is all unavoidable. Memories and dreams are a big chunk of what it means to be human.

But living in the past and the future doesn't make us happy. You have to take your happiness where you find it – in the smile of a loved one, in the blaze of a glorious sunset, in the moment you live in, the day you have now, the sandwich you are holding.

Easier said than done, of course, this enjoy-every-sandwich malarkey. But to expect happiness in anything else but the moment you are living in is to pin your wildest dream of smoke, mist and shadows.

The past can't make you happy. The future – that future when everything will be different, if only we get that new job, that kinder lover, that other life – can't make you happy. It's not real.

We are so bad at counting our blessings. We are so lousy at seeing the beauty of what is right in front of us. We miss the beauty of today because it is less than perfect.

Forget perfection. Forget a life with no bum notes. Forget – if you can – the dream of everything being transformed by the magic wand of something you do not have. Because it will not make you happy.

And to enjoy every sandwich, to live truly in the moment, to suck the juice out of every day we are given on this little blue planet, we have to accept something that is not very easy to accept.

Everything passes. All is transitory.

Enjoy every sandwich, every sunset and every smile because it all fades away. The good news is that even in the blackest night there are blessings to be counted, if only you can find them, if only you can have the courage to see that – no matter how hard life is, no matter how alone you feel – there are still these brief moments of happiness. They can be found anywhere – in the smell of a dog, the curve of a child's face, the shifting clouds, a piece of music that was created by someone who has been dead for fifty years.

No matter how hard life gets, you are alive – and happiness – tiny nuggets of happiness, perhaps, or even happiness that is invisible to the naked eye – is still there. It really is!

Being advised to enjoy every sandwich is not the same as being told to get a grip of yourself, or cheer up it might never happen, or go on give us a smile.

Enjoying every sandwich means finding a way to see that there are sparks of bright, shining light in even the most hopeless, darkest hours.

There have been times life has had me on my knees. The usual stuff. Nothing special. The same epic everyday events that derail any ordinary life. The death of a loved one. The fear of illness. The collapse of a relationship. And I know that if I had been able to enjoy every sandwich then my tears would not have been quite so bitter, and my heart would have known that it would heal in time. But nobody pretends that enjoying every sandwich is easy. It is, however, very necessary. Even the longest life is a short flicker of time – although it doesn't feel like that when life is slapping you down – and enjoying every sandwich is, in the end, our only hope.

Life hurts. All of us, in different measures and at different times. It's not fair. There is no justice. But nobody gets through a lifetime without pain, without getting hurt, and without wounds that they will carry to their grave.

This is the best I can offer you – we can all be happy, as long as we accept that all happiness is short-lived, and as long as we learn that we have to take our happiness where we find it. True happiness is a fragile, fleeting thing, and it can come at unexpected moments. The most difficult, but most rewarding skill you can learn is to recognise happiness when it is right there in front of you.

So enjoy every sandwich – if you can, if it's possible, if it takes you a lifetime, for I know that being told to enjoy every sandwich can be like being asked to levitate when the world is against you. But happiness is more than the absence of pain, and happiness is more than the memory of better days, and happiness is more than the yearning for a future moment that may never come.

Happiness is here for us today, if we dare to claim it, if only we can look beyond our past, our future and – yes – the unendurable pain of today, and salvage something real and precious and joyous from the moment we are living in.

Happiness is never a permanent state. You can't suddenly arrive there, as though it was a destination just beyond the edge of the A to Z. Even with all the happiness stalwarts in place – the work going well, the doctor's tests all clear, the family smiling, the sun shining – happiness still comes and goes. And the heartbreaker, the tragedy of all our lives, is that we so rarely recognise happiness even when it is there in front of us.

We spend years and years as slaves to the past and slaves to the future. Only a love of the present – no matter how fleeting, no matter how modest – can set us free. And give us the happiness we all deserve.

47. Tony Husband

Tony Husband has been a full-time cartoonist since 1984. His cartoons have appeared in many newspapers, magazines, books and websites, and in several TV and theatrical productions. *Yobs*, which he draws for *Private Eye*, is one of the best-known comic strips in Britain. He has won more than fifteen major awards, including the Pont Award for depicting the British way of life.

48. @Sectioned_

Under the pseudonym @Sectioned_ (please remember the underscore at the end, otherwise you'll be reading about a club night in Huddersfield), she tweets on mental health topics including inpatient and community care and media representations of mental ill-health, as well as hashtags such as #pillshaming and #headclutcher. In 2014, her blog sectioneduk.wordpress.com was shortlisted for the Mind Media Awards.

When I said to my friend, 'I've been asked to write a letter to a stranger about . . . happiness. What can I say?' she replied, 'But I want . . . a penis. Everybody wants . . . a penis. But you cannot hold . . . a penis. It's elusive. You cannot touch . . . a penis.' It's a quote from the film *Hector and the Search for Happiness*, which we'd watched the night before, when a heavily accented woman had approached psychiatrist Hector, mispronouncing 'happiness' as 'a penis'. We giggled.

Happiness can, indeed, be elusive (though giggling about dangly bits can help). For my friend, the secret was to find happiness in what she had, and not compare herself to others. For me, it was about finding happiness where I could – even on a locked ward, where I'd had a pretty toxic experience of in-patient psychiatric care.

The familiar 'one in four' statistic belies the fact that hardly any of us will ever go on to a locked psychiatric ward, whether as patient, visitor or professional. So I thought I'd shine a light on my experience of that closed world and share that, even in awful circumstances, it's possible to find happiness. For instance, I found happiness in:

- Baths – The ward was not short of bathrooms and, although the ones at the far end of the L-shaped ward stank of fags and weed and were where the girl gang that bullied me would hang out, I found one nearer the nurses' station which was large and clean. Twice a day, I'd set up camp there and bathe, imagining myself in a luxury spa. I'd use a ward-issue giant sanitary towel to stick across the plughole (there were no plugs), keep topping up with warm water and drench myself using a big plastic yoghurt tub. A cabin crew friend kept me supplied with luxury mini-toiletries. Immersed in warm water, bathing was a source of pleasure and relaxation for me.

- Visits from friends and family – These were my mainstay. I had visitors every day, sometimes several times a day. Connection with people who knew me well helped me cling on to my sense of self – of 'me' – in a place where it felt my identity had been stripped away by staff indifference, callousness and tick-box monitoring. I don't know how the patients I read about in the news, who are shipped halfway across the country because there are no local beds, can manage.

- Birthday cake – On my birthday, I received four different birthday cakes. There was cake for everyone on the ward that night. It was, despite the surroundings, one of my best birthdays ever. Not just because of the cake, candles and the four rounds of Happy Birthday to You that were sung to me: friends and family made the difference. Oh, and all the gifts they brought.

- Plants – People brought me all sorts of indoor plants and I had them lined up on the windowsill beside my bed space. Tending them carefully, the greenery was a reminder of nature and that there was life beyond the oppressive ward walls.

- The view from one of the windows – In the distance, I could see a tower block that I knew was on the edge of a big park. I'd look at that tower block and imagine myself in that big park, absorbing the moment, imagining the feeling of grass under my feet and the breeze on my face. Imagining the cool imprint on my soles helped me keep alive the possibility of freedom, even with no release date in sight.

- Being outside – After a few weeks restricted to the ward, I was allowed to join the smokers on their twice-daily supervised trips to the 'garden' – a rather grim smoking compound with a weather shelter in the centre surrounded by four storey-high walls and divided into two halves by a ten-foot wall. Women on one side of the high wall, men on the other, shouting over to each other, flirting, taunting, smoking. Being outside – feeling the breeze on my arms and the sunshine on my face – helped me to feel alive.

- Choosing food – Each day, we'd be handed a menu card from which we could choose up to seven items. I carefully chose my seven items. When your freedom, dignity and bodily integrity have been taken away, any aspect of your day where you're allowed choice becomes significant. Even though the food had no fibre (so everyone got constipated and put on weight), I would savour each item I'd chosen.

The ward was grim, there were too few staff (or too few good staff) and they rarely spoke to me, and I was what is euphemistically called 'nursed in seclusion' (locked up in solitary) and forcibly medicated (repeatedly). Overall, the experience was brutalising rather than healing (I refer to it as the Land That Human Rights Forgot). But still, even in that grim place, there were many moments of happiness. I had to look for them, but I did find them. They were the islands I hopped between.

So what I'm rambling towards saying is that, even in the darkest of places, there are moments of happiness, and they are worth clinging on to because they add up. These sparks of happiness helped me to get through everything else. And, in the end, I did get out. If you're staying on a locked psychiatric ward yourself, or if you know someone who is or who has been on such a ward then, in my experience, even if it's only brief moments, there are many opportunities for happiness. If you can, look for those moments yourself, or do what you can to help bring them to someone else. It's worth it.

49. Richard Layard

Professor Lord Richard Layard is a labour economist who has worked for most of his life on how to reduce unemployment and inequality. He is also one of the first economists to work on happiness, and his main current interest is how better mental health could improve our social and economic life. His concern with how to promote a happier society led him to co-found a new movement called Action for Happiness, where members from all backgrounds pledge to live so as to create as much happiness as possible.

Dear Stranger,

You do not know me nor I you. But, unless you are very
unusual, you almost certainly have a close relation or
friend who is suffering from mental health problems – or
has a child in serious distress. Typically people do not like
to talk about these things. It is seen as a sign of weakness
and shame – or, if you are a parent, as a failure.

But mental health problems are extremely common. At
this moment at least one adult in four is affected, and more
like two in five at some time in their lifetime. These mental
health problems come from the interaction of genes and
experience, and it is completely unhelpful to think of them
as anyone's fault. The good news is that they can now be
treated. The best treatments are all forward-looking, and
give people new skills to manage their negative thoughts
and emotions. In my opinion the best developed is
cognitive behavioural therapy (CBT) but there are others
which are equally effective.

These treatments are now becoming much more
available on the NHS. Until recently, you had to be
incredibly ill to get any psychological treatment for mental
health problems: often you had to be a physical danger to
yourself or someone else. So two thirds of those in need
got no treatment, not even medication. But since 2008 the
National Health Service has developed a completely new
service called Improving Access to Psychological Therapies

(IAPT). Unfortunately it has a different name in every part of the country, but you can find the name of your local service by going to the IAPT website.

A key point is that you can refer yourself directly to the service, without going through your GP. All the staff are well trained, and last year they treated 400,000 people. The service is of course not perfect, but it is improving rapidly in availability and quality.

And that is where you can help us. We want a service everywhere which is as easy to access as treatment for a broken leg. In other words, we want parity of esteem for mental and physical illness. But we are not there yet. The standard of service is uneven across the country and it currently sees on average only 15% of the 6 million adults with mental illness. Instead we want every service to see at least 25% by 2020.

This will only happen if there is enough local public pressure. So please go a second time to your computer and look up the performance of your local IAPT service on the website of Public Health (England). And if you are not satisfied with what you read, please write to your local Clinical Commissioning Group, complain to your GP, or write to the Health and Wellbeing Board of your local authority.

We need a society that is much more open about mental health problems; and the fact that these problems can now be treated makes this much easier. So if you are a supervisor or manager, please watch out for mental health

---

* Google 'Common mental health disorders profiling tool', then press 'Start – View Profile Data'. Select the 'CMHD Pathway' on the top tabs. For 'area type', select 'CCG' and then click 'Compare areas'. Then select your Commissioning region, your Area and your Indicator. (If you want, the resulting data can be ordered from high to low by pressing ▼ underneath Value.)

problems in your workforce (remember the figure of one in four). If people are underperforming, ask if they're OK and, if not, tell them about the opportunities for treatment. If they go off sick, ring them up and help ease their return to work.

It would be even better if we could prevent mental health problems in the first place. So, if you're a teacher, please read up on mental health and help campaigners like myself in our effort to get evidence-based life skills as a statutory part of the curriculum.*

For everybody there is always more we can do to improve our mental balance. Many people find mindfulness an extremely helpful practice and doing good is also a very healthy habit. Both these and more are passionately promoted by organisations such as Action for Happiness, of which I am one of the founding members.

Mental illness may not always be curable, but it can almost always be alleviated. It affects some 1–2% of the population – we must strive to reduce its impact even further in the future. That is a whole new world, and a much happier one.

Wherever you are, may you go well.

Yours,
Richard Layard

* If you want an idea of what 'evidence-based' means, go to the website of a programme called Developing Healthy Minds in Teenagers: www.howtothrive.org/healthy-minds.

50. Dave Chawner

Dave Chawner is an award-winning comedian who uses comedy to remove the stigma around mental health and eating disorders. Last year's critically acclaimed show *Over It*, which focussed on his nine-year battle with anorexia, toured the country and every major festival. As seen on the BBC, ITV and Channel 4, he 'makes you think as well as laugh' (Broadway Baby).

Dear Stranger,

Why are you reading this? You're looking for answers. We all are. I know I am. I found that I was looking in the wrong places.

I thought happiness was everything. I believed it was the be all and end all. It was a carrot dangling on a stick. Happiness motivated, excited and comforted me. If I could be happy I could be anything. It was a kind of body armour, that Friday feeling any day of the week. To me happiness was my favourite song coming on the radio, the last day of school, finding a forgotten fiver in old jeans. I thought happiness was everything but I found something better – contentment.

It sounds ridiculous but it is really obvious. Think of the happiest moment of your life. Go on, try. Maybe it is when you met your partner. Perhaps it is when you achieved something, went somewhere, saw someone. It could be romantic, exciting, unexpected. Whatever it is, think about it. *Really* think about it.

Got it?

Now, think about yesterday.

It probably wasn't as good, was it!? For every sunset there's a sunrise, for every heatwave there's a drought.

Happiness is fleeting. It comes and goes. So many things that we think make us happy have a shelf life – money, jobs, substances. Like a cat chasing a ball of string, it will eventually slip out of your grasp. Happiness is an emotion but contentment is a state.

What you really want is something stable, something sustainable and permanent. Happiness doesn't last. Being content does. It's a sip not a gulp. It is comforting, confident and caring. It takes everything into account. Contentment is a task not a result.

To be content is to be contained. It's an inward-facing smile. It is a hand on a shoulder. It's just for you without being selfish. It gets rid of fear, angst and intimidation. Yet it doesn't ask for more.

To be content is to be in the moment. This day, hour, minute is unique. Contentment makes the most of that. It lays out the possibility ahead while celebrating the victory trailing behind.

To be content is to be grateful. You become grateful for what you would otherwise take for granted. It makes you appreciate what you have not what you want. It stops you in your tracks. It opens up all everyday actions, words and thoughts. You find your sense of wonder.

And, who am I to tell you this? I'm not content every single moment of every single day? Of course not! It's not easy. If it was easy it wouldn't be worth it. I don't have all the answers. But I do have an aim – to be content. And I wish that for you too.

So, if you're looking for answers, I have none. But if you're looking for help, this is the place to start.

Dave Chawner

Useful Contacts

Mind
web: mind.org.uk
infoline: 0300 123 3393
email: info@mind.org.uk
text: 86463
legal advice line: 0300 466 6463
email: legal@mind.org.uk
online peer support community: elefriends.org.uk

**British Association for Counselling and
Psychotherapy (BACP)**
tel: 01455 883 300
web: bacp.co.uk

Carers UK
helpline: 0808 808 7777
web: carersuk.org

Samaritans
helpline: 0845 790 9090
email: jo@samaritans.org
web: Samaritans.org

Young Minds
parent helpline: 0808 802 5544
web: youngminds.org.uk

J. Levitin Rowan Coleman Helen Dun
xandra fuller Arianna Huffington Nick H
i Alderman Martha Roberts Giles Andrea
ton Yuval Noah Harari Genevieve Taylor
ancen Molloy-Vaughan Dave Chawner Nic
worthy Molly Pearce Richard Branson @
t Abbie Ross Richard Layard Philippa
s Pinnock John Lewis-Stempel Thomas H
niel J. Levitin Rowan Coleman Helen D
Alexandra fuller francesca Martinez Ni
aomi Alderman Martha Roberts Giles And
Burton Yuval Noah Harari Genevieve Tay
Molloy-Vaughan Dave Chawner Edward
y Molly Pearce Richard Branson Ellen
ie Ross Sathnam Sanghera Philippa Rice
nock John Lewis-Stempel Thomas Hardi
J. Levitin Rowan Coleman Helen Dunm
ndra fuller Arianna Huffington Nick Ha
Alderman Martha Roberts Giles Andrea
on Yuval Noah Harari Richard Layard Ch
ancen Molloy-Vaughan Jo Elworthy Edward
hy Molly Pearce Richard Branson @Sectio
bbie Ross Sathnam Sanghera Philippa Rice